Complementarity Between Lexis and Grammar in the System of Person

This book investigates the lexicogrammatical complementarity in language in its construal of person as a semantic system. Given the vast and wide spectrum of resources for expressing distinctions in the assignment of person roles in language, this book presents person-related system networks covering a rich range of semantic features. It also studies the system of person in relation to other major semantic systems instead of regarding it as one isolated component of language parallel to gender, number, case, etc. Systemic features of person are in turn realized by lexicogrammar, whose components, lexis and grammar, form a relationship of complementarity in the process of transforming human experience into meaning. Person-related meaning can be realized by either lexical means (i.e. entity, process, quality) or grammatical means (i.e. pronouns, clitics, affixes, zero forms). Besides, such meaning is also found to be realized at some indeterminate areas along the lexis-grammar continuum. A special feature of this book is that it observes the lexicalization and grammaticalization of person based on evidence from a variety of languages. Readers will be presented with a comprehensive look into the meaning of person and will be encouraged to reflect on its realization in their own languages.

Pin Wang is lecturer in the School of Foreign Languages at Shanghai Jiao Tong University in China, teaching English and Sanskrit. His research interests are Systemic Theory, Functional Grammar and Functional Language Typology, with particular focus on classical languages (e.g. Sanskrit) and minority languages of China (e.g. Tibetan).

China Perspectives Series

The *China Perspectives* series focuses on translating and publishing works by leading Chinese scholars, writing about both global topics and China-related themes. It covers Humanities & Social Sciences, Education, Media and Psychology, as well as many interdisciplinary themes.

This is the first time any of these books has been published in English for international readers. The series aims to put forward a Chinese perspective, give insights into cutting-edge academic thinking in China, and inspire researchers globally.

For more information, please visit https://www.routledge.com/series/CPH

Complementarity Between Lexis and Grammar in the System of Person
A systemic typological approach
Pin Wang

Forthcoming titles

The Use of L1 Cognitive Resources in L2 Reading by Chinese EFL Learners
Wu Shiyu

On Aesthetic and Cultural Issues in Pragmatic Translation
Feng Xiuwen

Assessing Listening for Chinese College English Learners
Developing a Communicative Listening Comprehension Test Suite for CET
Pan Zhixin

Patterns and Meanings of Intensifiers in Chinese Learner Corpora
Wang Chunyan

Language Policy
A Systemic Functional Linguistic Approach
Yang Bingjun & Wang Rui

A Corpus Study of Collocation in Chinese Learner English
Lu Yuanwen

Complementarity Between Lexis and Grammar in the System of Person
A systemic typological approach

Pin Wang

First published 2017
by Routledge
2 Park Square, Milton Park, Abingdon, Oxon OX14 4RN

and by Routledge
711 Third Avenue, New York, NY 10017

*Routledge is an imprint of the Taylor & Francis Group,
an informa business*

© 2017 Pin Wang

The right of Pin Wang to be identified as author of this work has been asserted by him in accordance with sections 77 and 78 of the Copyright, Designs and Patents Act 1988.

All rights reserved. No part of this book may be reprinted or reproduced or utilised in any form or by any electronic, mechanical, or other means, now known or hereafter invented, including photocopying and recording, or in any information storage or retrieval system, without permission in writing from the publishers.

Trademark notice: Product or corporate names may be trademarks or registered trademarks, and are used only for identification and explanation without intent to infringe.

British Library Cataloguing in Publication Data
A catalogue record for this book is available from the British Library

Library of Congress Cataloging-in-Publication Data
Names: Wang, Pin (Lecturer in languages) author.
Title: Complementarity between lexis and grammar in the system of person : a systemic typological approach / Pin Wang.
Description: London ; New York : Routledge, [2017] | Includes bibliographical references and index.
Identifiers: LCCN 2016014100 | ISBN 9781138204416 (hbk) | ISBN 9781315469294 (ebk)
Subjects: LCSH: Grammar, Comparative and general—Person. | Grammar, Comparative and general—Grammar. | Grammar, Comparative and general—Complement. | Lexicology. | Systemic grammar. | Typology (Linguistics)
Classification: LCC P240.85 .W26 2016 | DDC 415/.5—dc23
LC record available at https://lccn.loc.gov/2016014100

ISBN: 978-1-138-20441-6 (hbk)
ISBN: 978-1-315-46929-4 (ebk)

Typeset in Times New Roman
by Apex CoVantage, LLC

Printed and bound in Great Britain by
TJ International Ltd, Padstow, Cornwall

Contents

Figures and tables vi
Acknowledgments viii
Abbreviations ix

1 Introduction 1

2 Systemic theories and lexicogrammar 10

3 Person as a system 29

4 Lexicalization and grammaticalization of person 57

5 Complementarity between lexis and grammar: a systemic functional perspective 85

6 Conclusion 104

Bibliography 110
Index 118

Figures and tables

Figures

2.1	MOOD system in English	16
2.2	System network of MOOD	18
2.3	Stratification and realization	21
2.4	Extended stratification	22
3.1	System network of SUBJECT: person	30
3.2	Subsystem of nominality vs. pronominality	31
3.3	Subsystem of nominality vs. pronominality (extended)	32
3.4	Subsystem of DISCOURSE ROLE	34
3.5	System of person featuring NOMINALITY and DISCOURSE ROLE	34
3.6	Subsystem of NUMBER	37
3.7	Subsystem of INCLUSIVENESS	38
3.8	Subsystem of INCLUSIVENESS (extended to incorporate plurality)	39
3.9	System network of English pronouns in the nominative case	40
3.10	System of person featuring DISCOURSE ROLE, NUMBER and GENDER	41
3.11	System of first person plural featuring GENDER and INCLUSIVENESS	41
3.12	System of person featuring interaction of GENDER, NUMBER and CASE	43
3.13	Extended classification of pronominals	46
3.14	Subsystem of EMPHASIS	48
3.15	Emphatic person forms in English	48
3.16	Subsystem of HONORIFICATION	50
3.17	Referential demonstratives in English	51
3.18	Referential demonstratives in Japanese	52
3.19	Synthesized system of person	55
4.1	Vocative vs. non-vocative nominal participant	64

Figures and tables vii

4.2	Nominal-pronominal continuum	79
4.3	English/Chinese/Japanese pronouns on the pronominality scale	82
5.1	Complementarity of metafunctions	88
5.2	Complementarity of axis	88
5.3	Complementarity of agnation	89
5.4	Complementarity of perspective	90
5.5	Complementarity of semogenesis	91
5.6	SFL metalinguistic resources	91
5.7	Complementarity between lexis and grammar	93
5.8	Relexicogrammaticalization	95
6.1	Topological representation of person-related features	108

Tables

2.1	Realization statements	15
2.2	Notation for system networks	17
3.1	Elements of a nominal group	32
3.2	Possible groups of participants	38
3.3	Gender-related phonological/orthographical saliency	40
3.4	Case paradigm of the Latin noun *servus*	42
3.5	Classification of genitive personal pronouns	45
3.6	German personal pronoun paradigm	50
4.1	Honorific and humble verbs in Japanese	67
4.2	Person-indicating suffixes for the Latin verb *vocō*	74
4.3	A summary of the participant roles in Example 4.22	78
5.1	Disparities in locations on the lexis-grammar continuum	95

Acknowledgments

I would like to acknowledge my substantial debt to my PhD supervisor, Professor Zhu Yongsheng, who introduced me to the vast knowledge of Systemic Functional Linguistics and offered me active encouragement in my academic studies. I gained considerable enlightenment through attending his lectures, opening up discussions with him and seeking his guidance in various other ways. During the preparation and writing of this book, Professor Zhu provided many insightful suggestions and comments, without which this work would never have been possible.

I would also like to express my heartfelt gratitude to Professor James R. Martin at the Department of Linguistics, University of Sydney. During my scholarly visit there, I benefited much from his lectures and drew many inspirations from his biweekly individual supervision hours. It was also an invaluable experience to have participated in the Sydney typology seminars under the leadership of Professor Martin.

I am grateful to Professor Zhang Delu from Tongji University, Professor Wang Zhenhua from Shanghai Jiao Tong University and Professor Zheng Lixin from Shanghai Maritime University for subjecting the first draft of this book to rigorous scrutiny and offering cogent advice and suggestions for its improvement.

My thanks also go to Professor Chu Xiaoquan and Professor Qu Weiguo at Fudan University, who put forward precious ideas on specific parts of this book when I initially submitted my writing plan for this book as my PhD dissertation.

Finally, I would like to give special acknowledgment to Professor Ma Weilin from Changshu Institute of Technology, who proofread the draft of this book and alerted me to some inadvertent mistakes and ambiguities in language.

Abbreviations

ABL	Ablative case
ACC	Accusative case
AGR	Agreement
AGT	Agent
BEN	Beneficiary
CIRC	Circumstance
CLT	Clitic
DAT	Dative case
DIR	Directional
DU	Dual
EMPH	Emphatic
EXCL	Exclusive
EXM	Exclamation
F	Feminine gender
GEN	Genitive case
NOM. GP.	Nominal group
HON	Honorific
IMP	Imperative
INCL	Inclusive
INT	Interrogative
LOC	Locative case
M	Masculine gender
N	Neuter gender
NEG	Negation
NOM	Nominative case
PAR	Participant
PASS	Passive
PAST	Past tense
PERF	Perfective aspect
PL	Plural
PRES	Present tense
PROG	Progressive aspect

PROJ	Projection
RECP	Reciprocal
REFL	Reflexive
SG	Singular
TMP	Temporal
TOP	Topic
VOC	Vocative case
1	First person
2	Second person
3	Third person

1 Introduction

1.1 An overview of person

The concept of person as a fundamental facet of human experience has been extensively discussed in many domains of study such as philosophy, anthropology, sociology, psychology and philology. It has attracted close attention particularly in linguistics since it is an inextricable component of human language. Where there is human consciousness of distinction between one's self and others, the notion of person exists. Therefore, there is no doubt about the universality of person forms in language, which embodies humans' construal of the world. "A language without the expression of person cannot be imagined" (Benveniste, 1971: 225).

In language, person is incarnated as the deictic reference to a participant in a speech event; i.e. it identifies and differentiates speech roles involved in an utterance. The addresser of an utterance is known as the first person, the addressee of the utterance the second person, and the party referred to that is neither the addresser nor the addressee the third person. According to Lyons (1977: 638), "there is a fundamental, and ineradicable, difference between the first and second person, on the one hand, and the third person on the other." This notion is unquestionably derived on the ground that the first and second persons are directly involved in the speech event, while the third person is not an immediate participant in the speech act but a mere referent that could be either present or absent.

This difference is demonstrated in language in that the first and second persons are commonly realized essentially by personal pronouns whereas the third person can be fulfilled by virtually any lexical item. Some languages may have only first and second person markers and lack third person ones. In Latin, for example, there are only first and second person personal pronouns in principle, the singular and plural nominative forms being *ego, tū, nōs, vōs* (I, you SG, we, you PL) respectively. The nominative forms of third person markers in Latin are:

is	3 M SG	"he"
ea	3 F SG	"she"
id	3 N SG	"it"
eī/iī	3 M PL	"they"
eae	3 F PL	"they"
ea	3 N PL	"they"

The third person forms *is, ea, id, eī/iī, eae, ea* are in origin demonstrative pronouns (this, that; these, those), and the demonstratives are still in use as either pronouns or adjectives, as in Example 1.1:

Example 1.1 Demonstrative as third person pronoun in Latin

is vir "this man"
eae feminae "these women"

There are many other languages that lack person markers for the third person, and reference to the third person is achieved by demonstrative pronouns or solely specific nominal expressions. In yet other languages there is no overt expression at all for the third person, with the absence of an explicit expression being inferred as denoting the third person (see Forchheimer, 1953: 6; Siewierska, 2004: 5–6).

The fundamental distinction between the first and second person, on the one hand, and the third person, on the other, is attributed to the former's dependence on the discourse. That is to say, the reference of the first and second person forms, most prominently first and second person pronouns, is determined by the alternate discourse roles, whereas the reference of the third person is generally fixed. This is illustrated in the following simple conversation, in which the first person pronoun *I* (*me*) refers to person A and person B respectively. Likewise, the referent of *you* is person B in the first utterance and person A in the other. However, the referent of *she* remains unchanged for both utterances.

Example 1.2 Alternate discourse roles of first and second person pronouns

A: **I** must tell **you** that she doesn't love **you**.
B: **I** don't believe **you**. She loves **me**.

In contrast to the above dichotomy of person, there is another position of person dichotomy which groups the second and third person together in opposition to the first person, assuming that the fundamental person distinction is between speaker and non-speaker. This position is mainly espoused by Grasserie (1888: 3) and van Ginneken (1907: 211). Their idea is echoed by Boas with his statement:

> Logically, our three persons . . . are based on the two concepts of self and not-self, the second of which is subdivided, according to the needs of speech, into the two concepts of person addressed and person spoken of.
> (Boas, 1911: 39–40)

A number of linguistic studies, especially on American Indian languages and Baltic-Finnic languages (Akmajian & Anderson, 1970; Delisle, 1973; Booij et al., 2004; Fleck, 2008), advocate that there is a fourth person in some languages. As a matter of fact, the "fourth person" merely refers to some special cases of the third person, such as the impersonal form, the passive form, the reflexive form, or some other less commonly used third person inflections. Indeed, the so-called fourth person should not stand as an additional person type since it by no means qualifies as a separate role in a discourse event. Therefore, the taxonomy involving a fourth person is not adopted in the present study.

In opposition to the addition of a fourth person, some linguists seek to cut down the number of person contrasts from three to two. They contend that the third person is actually a non-person because, unlike the first and second person, it is not an immediate participant in a speech act. This view is most eminently held by Wundt (1911), Bloomfield (1933) and Benveniste (1971). However, this book does not accept this argument but entirely endorses the justifiable position of the third person as a person category in language relative to the first and second persons.

There are other person distinctions in language such as singular vs. plural, e.g. *I* vs. *we*; masculine vs. feminine, e.g. *he* vs. *she*; animate vs. inanimate, e.g. *he/she* vs. *it*; honorific vs. intimate, e.g. German *Sie* vs. *du*; inclusive *we* vs. exclusive *we*; non-reflexive vs. reflexive, e.g. *you* vs. *yourself*; non-possessive vs. possessive, e.g. *I* vs. *my*; and so on. And there are also socially and stylistically varied uses of person forms that contain information encoded within different means of expression to indicate social status, familiarity/distance, relationships, stylistic characteristics, etc. relevant to the participant roles.

1.2 Person as a grammatical category

"Category" is a general term used in linguistics at different levels of abstraction. It can reflect various processes of organizing human experience into general concepts with their associated linguistic labels. With regard to grammar, it refers to the established set of classificatory properties or units adopted in the description of language which occur as a structural paradigm throughout the language. "Grammatical category" has been used to cover a wide range of things, such as what is called in traditional grammar a "part of speech." More specifically, however, a grammatical category means a set of defining features, i.e. syntactic features, of the general units that express meaning from the same conceptual domain and that manifest in contrast to each other. For example, the categories of nouns consist of number, gender, case, countability, definiteness, etc.; those of verbs include tense, aspect, voice, mood, modality, transitivity, etc. And the category of person can be expressed in, but is not limited to, the finite use of verbs.

Interestingly, word classes like nouns and verbs can be defined the other way round in some languages. Pei (2007: 39–40) reports that in descriptive linguistics on Sanskrit, instead of saying nouns have certain grammatical categories, linguists maintain that it is words with grammatical categories of gender, number, case and voice that are identified as nouns. Thus, what are commonly known as adjectives also fall into the class of nouns simply because they share the same grammatical categories. Likewise, verbs are usually defined as words used to describe actions or occurrences, but, in Sanskrit, words that have grammatical categories of number, person, gender, case, tense, mood and voice are called verbs. In short, the grammatical categories a given word possesses determine its "part of speech."

That a grammatical category comprises syntactic features or options which express meaning from the same conceptual domain and manifest in contrast to each other makes it look like a "system" from the perspective of Systemic Functional Linguistics (hereafter sometimes abbreviated as SFL). This is indeed true. In his analysis of modern Chinese, Halliday (1956) establishes three types of grammatical categories in the description: unit, element and class. According to Halliday, the "unit" is a category that corresponds to a segment of the linguistic material about which statements are to be made, such as a sentence, clause, group, word or character in Chinese; the element and the class are categories designated to describe the unit. The "element" is structural and is stated with symbols; for example, in a clause with an ANV structure, A, N and V are elements occupying their corresponding positions in that clause structure. The "class" is paradigmatic in relation to the clause structure and operates at a particular place in the structure, such as "V: transitive/intransitive." Thus, the class is systemic and consists of exhaustive inventories of choices operating at a given place in the structure of a unit.

In order to establish a descriptive model for general linguistics, Halliday switched his focus of studies from Chinese to English in the 1960s and created an influential method of grammar description in "Categories of the Theory of Grammar" (1961). This paper is thus seen as the precursor of Scale and Category Grammar. The fundamental categories for the theory of grammar at this stage, according to Halliday, are four: unit, structure, class and system, with "element" dropping out and "structure" and "system" newly recruited. The four components of grammatical categories are interrelated to and derivable from each other.

The "unit" is the category which accounts for the stretches that carry grammatical patterns, ranging from the largest to the smallest. The units of grammar form a taxonomic hierarchy which may vary from language to language. For example, the units for the English language are the sentence, clause, group/phrase, word and morpheme.

The "structure" is the grammatical category set up to account for likeness between successivity; therefore, it is an abstraction of patterns of syntagmatic relations. A structure is made up of a series of elements represented phonologically or graphically as being in linear progression. Any structure is one of a given unit, and it naturally appears reasonable that the lowest unit carries no structure. If it did, there would be another unit below.

In contrast, the "class" accounts for the paradigmatic relations in the grouping of members of a particular unit. It is determined by the operation in the structure of the next unit above. In the reverse way, a structure is defined with reference to the classes of the next unit below. In short, all structures presuppose classes, and all classes presuppose structures. And both the structure and the class are variable in terms of delicacy.

What accounts for the occurrence of one item rather than another from a pool of choices is the "system". In the operation of a structure, as stated above, what enters into its grammatical relations is the class as an abstraction from a list of formal items, instead of the item itself. It logically leads to a system of the class, from which choices are made when an element in a given structure requires a certain class. Items in the system of the class are mutually exclusive and mutually determinative. Subsequently, Halliday viewed the system as of paramount importance in accounting for the operation of language among the grammatical categories. A more detailed review of systemic theories is to be given in the next chapter.

Halliday has expanded the scope of grammatical category, which, in its traditional sense, corresponds to the "system" in Halliday's model. Thus, it is entirely justifiable to call the person a system which is derived from the grammatical category in the first place. And, in a broader sense, the category of person can be embodied in a particular linguistic form that is simultaneously an exponent of a unit, an element of a structure, a class and a term in a system.

1.3 Objectives of the study

Person as a fundamental system in the organization and operation of language represents an important aspect of the meaning potential of language. It plays a role in each of the three metafunctions, i.e. ideational, interpersonal and textual functions. Meaningful choices need to be made on the basis of various factors when it comes to the selection of appropriate person forms, the various factors including discourse roles, number, gender, animacy, intimacy, reflexivity, possessiveness, social status and a number of others, as is briefly mentioned in Section 1.1. The system of person could be immensely complicated and necessarily consists of many subsystems. However, not many studies concerning the system of person are seen in SFL studies and publications. Unlike some other systems that have been delved into in greater depth, such as Mood (Halliday & Matthiessen, 2004: 135; Fawcett, 2009; Martin et al., 2010: 94), Transitivity and various processes included (Halliday & Matthiessen, 2004: 183, 209, 217; Matthiessen & Halliday, 2009: 59), Theme (Halliday & Matthiessen, 2004: 80), Tense (Halliday, 1994: 202–203; Halliday & Matthiessen, 2004: 340–342), Appraisal systems (Martin & White, 2005), Intonation (Halliday & Greaves, 2008), etc., the system of person merely draws occasional attention and is represented in simplistic system networks, as in those of Eggins (2004: 202), Halliday and Matthiessen (2004: 41), Hu (2006: 309), Hu et al. (2008: 53), and Hu and Ye (2010: 135), to name a few. Fawcett (1988) makes a more intricate systemic analysis of English personal pronouns. It is probably because of, not in spite of, the fundamentality of the concept of person that it is largely taken for granted and thus somehow overlooked in Systemic Functional Linguistics. In view of this, the first objective of the present study would be to try to provide a comprehensive analysis of person (in Chapter Three) against an SFL background, adopting in particular a kind of graphic representation called system networks.

SFL theories on stratification and realization suggest that semantic features are realized by lexicogrammar, which in turn is realized by phonology (or graphology), hence the three-stratum ordering of how language operates and functions. Traditionally it is maintained that vocabulary and grammar are two distinct orders of linguistic phenomena, and they are felt to require separate treatment.

6   *Introduction*

However, SFL holds that lexical items and grammar are not different ranks of language but two poles of a single unified continuum. It is systemic functional linguists' observation that lexis and grammar (properly combined as lexicogrammar) bear a relation of complementarity in the process of transforming human experience into meaning, although some other linguists also stand by the view that vocabulary and grammar are at the same level when it comes to the description of language.

The system of person, like all other semantic systems, is unexceptionally realized by lexicogrammar, which may manifest itself by either lexical or grammatical means. Moreover, the realization of person can even be spotted in the fuzzy areas along the lexis-grammar continuum. A large proportion of this study is intended to explore the lexical and grammatical realizations of the concept of person respectively, citing examples from a variety of natural languages apart from the more familiar English and Chinese. The ultimate purpose is to demonstrate how the seemingly discrete alternatives are meant to achieve the same end, i.e. the construal of human experience through meaningful units, via examination of the lexis-grammar complementarity displayed in the system of person.

A special emphasis needs to be made here that the term "person" in this book includes, but is by no means restricted to, personal pronouns. Personal pronouns definitely play a key role in identifying speech roles in discourses, but they do not represent the whole picture. "Person" in the present study refers to any means that serve to identify participant roles and impart participant information in discourse, including both lexical forms and grammatical forms (of which personal pronouns are a type), as has been briefly suggested above and will be amplified hereafter.

In summary, the principal issues to be addressed in this book are:

- Presentation of comprehensive and wide-ranging system networks for the category of person;
- Illustration of the lexicalization and grammaticalization of the system of person, a cross-linguistic study;
- Explication and interpretation of the complementarity between lexis and grammar with regard to person.

1.4   Organization of the book

This book consists of six chapters. The current chapter has established the objectives of study within the general theoretical framework of Systemic Functional Linguistics after providing a brief overview of the concept of person as a basic grammatical category.

Chapter Two gives a review of the existing achievements of studies and research concerning the topics under discussion. The literature review most notably focuses on systemic theories and the notion of lexicogrammar as a single unified stratum of language.

Chapter Three addresses the first objective listed above, i.e. the presentation of a detailed and comprehensive analysis of person in terms of systemic notation by using system networks. The system network for person is part of the wider-ranging networks of the meaning potential of language. Although there have been simplistic network representations of the system of person in systemic literature in which person is incorporated as part of the Mood structure of a clause, the realization of the concept of person involves a far more complex series of choices embodied by such features as discourse roles, number, gender, animacy, case, reflexivity, inclusiveness and so on. The system of person thus necessarily intersects with other systems.

Since the distinctions in the assignment of person roles in language can be expressed with a vast spectrum of resources, systemic analyses related to person need to be presented by covering a broader array of semantic features than the existing models do. This is the primary purpose of this chapter. Meanwhile, it observes the system of person in dynamic relation to other major semantic systems instead of regarding person simply as an isolated component of language parallel to gender, number, case, etc.

Chapter Four opens up discussions about the lexicalization and grammaticalization of the system of person. As will be argued in the chapter, the construal of the concept of person can rely either on the means of lexis or on those of grammar. It is exemplified in two sections of Chapter Four how the system of person can be realized through lexical and grammatical resources respectively. "Lexical resources" refers to the vocabulary, or lexicon, which primarily serves to denote substance (a.k.a. "entity" in SFL terminology), action (a.k.a. "process") and quality, such as nouns, verbs, adjectives and adverbs. Such lexical items are open-ended and in no way mutually defining; therefore, the lexical embodiment of person is by nature not meant to be made up of a closed set of lexis including all three speech roles, namely the first, second and third person. A lexical item can stand alone representing one speech role without necessarily suggesting the existence of the other two related to it. On the other hand, lexical items may be supplemented or removed non-systematically since their membership is in principle infinite and unfixed. Logically the lexis displaying features of person is also subject to addition and reduction.

"Grammaticalization" means the (process of) morphological realization of meaning by inflection and derivation, the sequential organization of structural elements, particles or other function words, etc. Person-related grammatical resources are those morphological forms employed in the construal of the concept of person, such as reduced and dependent forms, inflections and zero forms, as well as independent forms, i.e. personal pronouns. Compared with fully independent content words, the grammatical realization of the system of person mainly has three characteristics: (1) it is phonologically reduced; (2) it is morphologically dependent on other elements; and (3) it is semantically generalized.

Another section of this chapter is specially dedicated to the discussion of personal pronouns. In the practice of traditional grammar, pronouns are viewed as a morpho-syntactic category as separate from nouns. They are utilized as substitutes for nouns but differ from the latter in their morphological and syntactic properties. Pronouns are not capable of identifying a referent by themselves as nouns (both proper and common) do. They make up a closed and fixed set of expressions inherently, their members are mutually exclusive, and they are semantically generalized to a vast domain of application. Nonetheless, the distinction between pronouns and nouns is not so clear-cut as it seems to be. Sugamoto (1989) points out in a well-grounded analysis that certain personal pronouns exhibit fewer pronominal and more nominal features than others do, and vice versa. Accordingly, studies of personal pronouns on the pronominality-nominality cline are conducted in this section in a bid to reveal the multifaceted nature of this kind of person marker. What is more pertinent to the subject of study, the pronominality-nominality cline stands as solid evidence for the complementarity between lexis and grammar, a fundamental conception of language held by the SFL school.

Chapter Five presents a reasoned explication and interpretation of the relationship between lexis and grammar, which are held as constituting a unified stratum called lexicogrammar where meaning is transformed into wording. Lexis and grammar are complementary to each other as resources for expressing meaning, in the sense that lexis is regarded as the most delicate grammar, and grammar as the most general way of expressing meaning. The complementarity between lexis and grammar most effectively functions in their performance of the ideational function. That is to say, human experience can be construed through meaning either lexically or grammatically, or both lexically and grammatically at the same time. Each makes its own contribution to the whole picture of sense-making. The phenomena at one end are better explained with one conceptual framework, and those at the other end with another.

There are even more complex phenomena in the middle of the lexis-grammar continuum that are difficult to describe when vocabulary and syntax are taken as two separate levels of meaning organization. These phenomena can be interpreted either way because lexis and grammar are the two ends of a single continuum without a set boundary in the middle, so that the construal of meaning may occur at different points along this continuum, and, what is more, such phenomena may readily move from one place to another. The move is not one of rank but of delicacy. This accounts for the lexicalization and grammaticalization that take place both synchronically and diachronically.

From a typological point of view, the realization of the concept of person can resort to either lexical or grammatical means, and the construal of an identical person phenomenon can be found at different locations along the lexicogrammatical scale among different languages. The fact that personal pronouns manifest various degrees of pronominality also proves the unity and complementarity between lexis and grammar.

If a time line is drawn, person forms are subject to change along this line, too, though often regarded as one of the most stable parts of language. A large number of person expressions are believed to have originated from lexical items, the forms in use being the results of different degrees of grammaticalization. Others are from grammatical sources. This indication of delicacy migration along the lexis-grammar continuum again validates from a developmental perspective the complementarity in question.

Chapter Six brings what is discussed in the book to a conclusion. The system of person is realized in human language by means of lexicalization and grammaticalization, both of which are meaning-making strategies for the construal of experience. The complexity of the task of transforming human experience into meaning, and further into wording, demands such seemingly parallel but actually complementary approaches. Lexicogrammar as a unity provides language with semogenic power.

2 Systemic theories and lexicogrammar

2.1 Systemic Linguistics

Systemic Functional Linguistics (SFL), sometimes referred to as Systemic Functional Grammar, is a theory of language developed by M.A.K. Halliday. It is designed to be a comprehensive and holistic approach to language in context based on systems thinking (Matthiessen & Halliday, 2009: 8). SFL is composed of two parts: Systemic Linguistics and Functional Linguistics. "Functional" indicates that this model is more concerned with meaning and context than with the formal construction of linguistic units. The term "systemic" refers to a conception of language as a network of systems or interrelated sets of options for semogenesis. The system is conceived as the underlying principle of paradigmatic organization of language at any of the three strata, i.e. phonology, lexicogrammar and semantics.

Systemic Linguistics focuses on the resources or options that the grammar can provide to language users in generating meaning. The choices at various points enable the language users to convert their intentions into specific forms of language and, furthermore, to perform the intended functions. Halliday inherited this systemic view of language chiefly from Firth, and he was also influenced by other linguists or schools of linguistics such as Malinowski, the Prague School, Hjelmslev, Whorf, etc. In this section, a factual account of the development of Systemic Linguistics will be given, followed by some comments and criticism it has prompted.

2.1.1 Historical background: predecessors

Ferdinand de Saussure argues in his *Course of General Linguistics* that a linguistic sign is an entity related systematically to other linguistic signs to form a system, and the signifying features of the sign are determined by the way it is related to other signs (Saussure 1961/1960). He conceives of his notion of *langue* as bearing two kinds of relations: syntagmatic and associative (paradigmatic). All linguistic units are systematically related to other units by both kinds of relations. To Saussure, the system is the set of syntagmatic and associative relations that hold between the concrete entities of a *langue* (Hu & Ye, 2010: 54–55). In his structural approach, linearity, or syntagmatic relation, is paramount.

The notion of system was redefined by the European functionalists L. Hjelmslev and J. R. Firth. This subsection will focus on Hjelmslev, and Firth's idea of the system will be discussed in Section 2.1.2.

Hjelmslev (1953: 24) draws a binary distinction between "system" and "process" in language. A system is a correlational hierarchy with an underlying paradigmatic relation, while a process is a relational hierarchy with an underlying syntagmatic relation. This is reflected in his theory of language called glossematics.

Hjelmslev also draws a parallel among the relations between the items in each of the following pairs: system/process, text/language and syntagmatic/paradigmatic. The system is seen as the constant in semiotic function; therefore, language and paradigmatic relation shall also be viewed as constants or systems. In glossematicians' view, the scientific study and analysis of language ought to attach primary importance to the relations between linguistic elements rather than the physical properties of the elements.

The purpose of linguistic analysis, according to Hjelmslev, is to interpret linguistic features in terms of functions, instead of generalizing functions from the features. The spotlight is felt to fall equally on syntagmatic and paradigmatic relations; however, there is a clear comparability between paradigmatic relation and the notion of system.

Albeit a direct descendant from Hjelmslev and Firth, Halliday's systemic model is said to have been influenced by other linguistic schools like the Prague School and by B. L. Whorf's linguistic relativism. Halliday also recognizes points of contact with Lamb's stratificational grammar and with Pike's tagmemics (Butler, 1985: 4).

2.1.2 Firth on system

Firth voices opposition to Saussurean structuralism and regards Saussure's approach as monolithic. He is more concerned with description of languages for practical purposes. However, Firth's idea about language resembles Saussure's in that it is also built on the concept of syntagmatic and paradigmatic relations, which he views as two axes language is organized along.

Firth makes a distinction between structure and system. Elements in syntagmatic relation form "structures"; by "system", he refers to the paradigmatic association. The word "system" used here in this way has given rise to the term "systemic" featured in Hallidayan linguistics; Halliday acknowledges in his "Systemic Background" (1985b) that "it is from Firth . . . that the concept of system is derived, from which systemic theory gets its name." (1985b: 2)

The use of the term "system" in Firth's early works from the 1930s through the 1950s covers quite a broad range:

> Language and personality are built into the body, which is constantly taking part in activities directed to the conversation of the pattern of life. We must expect therefore that linguistic science will also find it necessary to postulate

the maintenance of linguistic patterns and systems (including adaptation and change) within which there is order, structure and function. Such systems are maintained by activity, and in activity they are to be studied. It is on these grounds that linguistics must be systemic.
(Firth, 1948, in Firth, 1957: 143)

The notion of system covering personal and social behaviors is later reduced to a "spectrum of linguistic techniques."

... [L]anguage is systemic. . . . "What is systemic?" We must not expect to find one closed system. But we may apply systematic categories to the statement of the facts. We must separate from the mush of general goings-on those features of repeated events which appear to be parts of a patterned process and handle them systematically by stating them by the spectrum of linguistic techniques. The systemic statements of meaning produced by such techniques need not be given existent status.
(Firth, 1950, in Firth, 1957: 187)

The use of the term "system" later becomes more specific and closer to paradigmatic relations:

... "[L]inguistic forms" are considered to have "meanings" at the grammatical and lexical levels, such "meanings" being determined by interrelations of the forms in the grammatical systems set up for the language.
(Firth, 1951, in Firth, 1957: 227)

Firth's view about system is seen by Palmer (1968: 7) as taking "from de Saussure (while rejecting much of de Saussure's theory) the notion of *value* (valeur)." However, the biggest difference between Firth's linguistics and Saussure's (and one of Firth's most significant contributions in linguistics) is that the former takes language as polysystemic as opposed to the latter's monosystemic view. Even within a single structure there could be several systems; and hardly any two systems are identical to each other.

Linguistic analysis must be polysystemic. For any given language there is no coherent system . . . which can handle and state all the facts.
(Firth, "Linguistic Analysis as a Study of Meaning," in Palmer, 1968: 24)

Firth's concepts of system and structure also extend to his studies of phonology. Firth finds the traditional phonemic approach to phonological description far from satisfactory, and so he proposes a method of analysis in terms of prosodies and phonematic units.

"Prosodies", according to Firth, are elements extending over phonological units to set the boundaries of particular structural divisions in a stretch of utterance. This concept of what is commonly known as suprasegmental features is basically structural (syntagmatic). "Phonematic units" are segmental units that result from the abstraction of prosodies. This notion is basically systemic (paradigmatic).

The polysystemic view of language is uniform with his view of context. The context of a particular linguistic element involves the other elements in paradigmatic relation. Halliday carries on with Firth's ideas on system and structure and establishes a linguistic theory in which the notion of system is made more explicit and upgraded to a prominent level.

2.1.3 Halliday's Systemic Linguistics

Following Firth's theoretical framework, Halliday argues that language is not composed of a set of grammatically correct sentences, and thus it cannot be explained with a set of rules but should be explained by its meaning potential instead. The description of language as a semiotic potential requires an investigation into sets of choices. This is the basis on which Systemic Grammar is established. Halliday's attempt to build a Systemic Grammar can be traced back to the 1950s and early 1960s in his studies of "Scale and Category Grammar," which is commonly recognized as the initial stage of Systemic Linguistics.

2.1.3.1 Scale and Category Grammar

As previously mentioned in Section 1.2, Halliday (1956) devises three basic grammatical categories, viz. unit, element and class, in his earliest theoretical framework, which need not be repeated here. In addition, he echoes Firth's emphasis on the context of situation, differentiates "given" and "new" information and fosters a probabilistic view for systemic options, all of which laid a foundation for the improved version of his linguistic theories afterward.

Further developments were made and can be found in Halliday (1961), where "system" is looked at as one of the four fundamental categories of grammar (unit, structure, class and system). This notion is established to account for "the occurrence of one rather than another from a number of like events" (Halliday, 1961: 264). A close system is a set of terms that have a finite number of members, each of which is exclusive to all the others, and if a new term is added to the system, the meaning of all the other terms would be changed. However, Halliday's notion of system at this stage is seen as "either too abstract or too sketchy to afford the uninitiated reader a sufficient grasp of the concept" (Butler, 1985: 27).

2.1.3.2 Systemic Grammar

The period from the mid-1960s to the early 1970s is a crucial phase in the development of Halliday's Systemic Grammar, with his article "Some Notes on 'Deep' Grammar" (1966) marking the outgrowth of Systemic Grammar from the previous scale and category model. Systems are now linked into networks with dependencies between different systems. Structure would appear as the realization of various systemic features.

2.1.3.2.1 SYSTEM

Halliday suggests that systems represent deep paradigmatic relations and embody sets of options available in a given functional environments. And the term "system" is glossed informally as "deep paradigm." The systemic description stands for a selection from among the possibilities recognized by the grammar.

The most significant leap forward in the development of Systemic Linguistics is that Halliday now states that paradigmatic relations are in fact primary because they constitute the fundamental underlying principles of language organization.

> ... it might be useful to consider some possible consequences of regarding systemic description as the underlying form of representation, if it turns out that the structural description could be shown to be derivable from it. In that case structure would be fully predictable, and the form of a structural representation could be considered in the light of this.
>
> (Halliday, 1966: 62)

Apart from placing system in the paramount position in the theory, Halliday also recognizes that systemic terms are closely related to their underlying semantic properties. This reflects his insistence on the meaningfulness of linguistic units and choices made in building these units.

> ... underlying grammar is semantically significant grammar. ... [T]hat part of the grammar which is as it were "closest to" the semantics may be represented in terms of systemic features. This would provide a paradigmatic environment for the "relatedness" of linguistic items, a contrast being seen as operating in the environment of other contrasts.
>
> (Halliday, 1966: 62–63)

2.1.3.2.2 REALIZATION

Halliday's term "realization" is believed to be borrowed from Lamb, to denote the derivation from systemic choices to the final formation of grammatical structures. It is generally a symbolic relationship between the content plane and the expression plane and may be otherwise termed as "expression," "coding," etc.

Halliday (1969: 82) specifies some realization rules, or statements, which are specifications of a structure fragment, such as the presence of a certain structural function, the ordering of one function with respect to another, and the conflation of two functions into a single element of structure. A realization statement is presented as a reexpression of a systemic feature or a combination of features. It consists of a realization operator (insert, conflate, expand, order and preselect) and one or more operands, at least one of which is a grammatical function. Table 2.1 shows the major types of realization statements and relevant examples.

Table 2.1 Realization statements (Matthiessen & Halliday, 2009: 98)

Major type	Operator	Operand 1	Operand 2	Example
(i) structuring	insert (+)	function	–	+Subject
	expand (( ))	function	function	Mood(Subject)
	order (^)	function	function	Subject^Finite
(ii) layering	conflate (/)	function	function	Subject/Agent
(iii) inter-rank realization	preselect (:)	function	feature(s)	Subject: nom. gp.

2.1.3.3 Characteristics of a system

A closed system consists of a set of options, each of which comprises two or more terms represented by features. A system has the following characteristics:

(1) Each system has its boundary; i.e. the number of terms is finite. For example, the system of gender in German includes three terms: masculine, feminine and neuter. However, the number of terms in a system is subject to change in accordance with changes in the language ipso facto. The system of gender in Swedish used to comprise three terms, i.e. masculine, feminine and neuter. Now in modern Swedish the masculine and feminine are grouped together as the common gender, so that the number of terms in this system has been reduced to two.

(2) In a system, each term is exclusive of all the others. When one term is selected, all the other terms are automatically forsaken. For example, the tense system in English is composed of three terms – present, past and future. If a clause adopts the present tense, it cannot simultaneously take either the past or the future tense.

(3) The terms under one system fall within the same semantic field. Each option in a system is one in terms of meaning. Only those concepts pertaining to the same semantic field can be brought together to constitute a system. Present, past and future are taken together to form the system of tense in that they all indicate the time of the action in relation to the time of utterance.

(4) The meaning of one term is dependent on the other terms in the same system. Self-evidently, if one term is added to or removed from the system, it necessarily alters the meaning of the other term(s). For example, there are three terms in the system of number in Old English: singular, dual and plural. However, there are only two in Modern English: singular and plural. Thus, the term "plural" carries different meanings in the original number system and the changed one, indicating "three or more" and "two or more" respectively.

(5) A system can be presented according to various degrees of delicacy, a scale from general to specific. Delicacy corresponds to the ordering of the system

16 *Systemic theories and lexicogrammar*

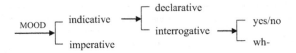

Figure 2.1 MOOD system in English

and its subsystems from left to right in a system network. For example, the systems of MOOD in English increase in delicacy from left to right (Figure 2.1).

2.1.3.4 System network

A system network is the notational convention which is established to capture the paradigmatic relations in the system. A system network is always read from left to right. It starts with an entry condition which specifies where the option is available, as well as a set of two or more terms, from which one and only one must be selected. And each term may have one or more realization statements associated with it. There is a set of graphic symbols to represent various relations (Table 2.2).

A system network of MOOD in English is illustrated in Figure 2.2.

2.1.4 Hudson's systemic syntax

R. A. Hudson is more widely recognized as a sociolinguist; however, he has made substantial contributions to Systemic Grammar as well, especially through his publications in the 1960s and 1970s. Hudson's systemic theory is directly derived from Halliday's model but has a distinctive character of its own, incorporating many ideas from transformational generative approaches to language. His systemic model deals specifically with the syntactic properties of linguistic units.

Hudson's systemic models comprise three major stages. In his *English Complex Sentences: An Introduction to Systemic Grammar* (1971), Hudson classifies grammatical units in the form of system networks to indicate paradigmatic relations. From the selection expression ("entry condition" in Halliday's term) of the systemic features of a linguistic item, a structure for that item is established by means of a set of structure-generating rules. He argues that every grammatical constituent bears some function. This model is primarily used to account for complex sentences in English.

The second stage is known as the "systemic generative grammar" model (Hudson, 1974). The main difference from the earlier account is that explicit inclusion of function labels is entirely dispensed with. Functional properties are instead derived by interpreting configurations of features.

The third-stage model makes explicit the dependency relations rather than leaving them implicit in either functional relations or configurations of features.

Table 2.2 Notation for system networks (based on Matthiessen & Halliday, 2009: 98, with revisions)

Diagram	Description
a → [x / y]	**system:** if "a," then "x" or "y"
a/b → [x / y]	**disjunction in entry condition:** if "a/b," then "x/y"
a,b → [x / y]	**conjunction in entry condition:** if "a" and "b," then "x/y"
a { → [x/y], → [m/n] }	**simultaneity:** if "a," then simultaneously "x/y" or "m/n"
a → [x / y] → [m / n]	**delicacy ordering:** if "a," then "x/y"; if "x," then "m/n"
a { → [x*→/y], → [m→*/n] }	**conditional marking:** if "x," then also "m"
a → [x/y], → [‖ "go on"]	**recursive system (logical):** if "a," then "x/y" and simultaneously the option of entering and selecting from the same system again
→ x/y/z (scale)	**scaled system:** a continuous scale extending from "x" through "y" to "z," with various intermediate points possible between "x" and "z"
↘	**realization**

The new model is a combination of elements from dependency grammars and his previous systemic models and is named "daughter dependency grammar."

Since the 1980s, Hudson has developed his grammatical theory in a new direction, which he calls "word grammar." This model is no longer regarded as systemic and thus marks a rupture with his earlier works.

18 *Systemic theories and lexicogrammar*

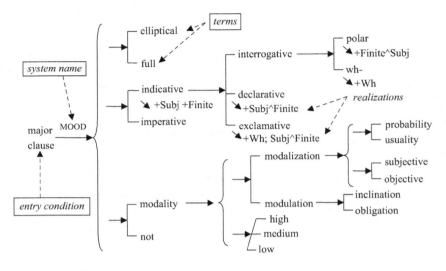

Figure 2.2 System network of MOOD (adapted from Eggins, 2004: 199)

2.1.5 *Fawcett's application and extension of systemic theory*

As a prominent systemicist R. P. Fawcett has exercised the systemic theory in the description of some aspects of the English language. Fawcett (1988) offers an instructive discussion on the English personal pronouns using system networks. He particularly espouses the integration of both semantic and formal criteria when explaining a linguistic choice. In his further elaboration of the semantic system behind the English personal pronouns, Fawcett contends that a semantic system is built to account not for all meanings in a language but for the meaning potentials in the organization of language.

In view of Halliday's failing to present system networks in the first two editions of *An Introduction to Functional Grammar*, Fawcett has been committed to making the systemic applications publicly available to a general readership. A systemic account of the English mood system is given in exquisite detail in Fawcett (2009), and many more accounts are expected in Fawcett (forthcoming a, b).

To extend Halliday's SFL, Fawcett and his colleagues have been working on the Cardiff Grammar, as an alternative to the Sydney Grammar. It combines the description of language in terms of meaning and function with its description in terms of form. He holds that some of the formally oriented approaches are "valuable in identifying the data of syntactic structures whose relationship to meaning requires careful modeling" (Fawcett, 2008: 18).

Cardiff Grammar attaches importance to both syntax and semantics, in that for each bit of language that it examines, the general pattern is "to work from the relatively observable phenomena at the level of form to the less directly observable phenomena at the level of meaning" (Fawcett, 2008: 34). It develops a framework at both levels that is designed to be implemented for describing languages per se and the texts that are produced in those languages, especially in a modern, computerized environment.

2.1.6 Matthiessen's contributions to Systemic Linguistics

While most of the publications on SFL have been centered on the functional aspect, C.M.I.M. Matthiessen has made great contributions to the systemic description of language. His main works on Systemic Linguistics include *Systemic Linguistics and Text Generation: Experiences from Japanese and English* (1991, co-authored with J. Bateman) and *Lexicogrammatical Cartography: English Systems* (1995).

Matthiessen also contributed to Halliday's third edition of *An Introduction to Functional Grammar* (2004), mostly in terms of the addition of systemic theory and system networks. Systemic theory is given more prominence in the rewritten first chapter and the largely revised second chapter. There are only three system networks in the first two editions of the book, while in the third edition the number is increased to 27, so that the important SFL theory "scale of delicacy" is more explicitly presented.

2.1.7 Other systemicists' contributions

Other prominent scholars in the field of Systemic Linguistics include, but are not limited to, J. Benson, W. S. Greaves, M. J. Cummings, M. Berry and C. S. Butler. They have brought the systemic thoughts into comprehensive and extensive introductions and reviews, or made them applicable to linguistic analyses.

Benson and Greaves edited a collection of papers (1985) on the systemic theory and its application that had been submitted to the ninth International Systemic Workshop. Three years later, Cummings joined them in editing another collected work on Systemic Linguistics.

Berry is known for presenting two important volumes of an introduction to Systemic Linguistics, namely *Introduction to Systemic Linguistics: 1, Structures and Systems* (1975) and *Introduction to Systemic Linguistics: 2, Levels and Links* (1977), which are the first comprehensive synthesis of systemic ideas.

So far, the book that best satisfies the need for an overview of the whole systemic field, describing and comparing the various systemic models put forward by Halliday and others, might be Butler's *Systemic Linguistics: Theory and Applications* (1985). It examines the roots of systemic theory, observes the development of Halliday's ideas and then discusses systemic approaches to other types of linguistic patterning; moreover, it deals with descriptions of English and other languages based on systemic models, and considers applications of systemic theories in areas like stylistics, education and artificial intelligence.

2.1.8 Criticisms of Systemic Grammar

It is beyond any doubt that Systemic Linguistics has offered a very enlightening perspective on the organizing and functioning of language and has made significant contributions to language teaching, stylistic analysis, computerized linguistic studies, artificial intelligence, etc. In spite of this, it has also met with some criticisms, most of which have come from within the circle of systemic linguists. Some major criticisms are as follows:

> Halliday's semantic networks are regarded as encoding behavioral options ("can do") in linguistic options ("can mean") and the meaning potential is connected with social contexts. Fawcett objects that the least delicate options are not necessarily realized through language, that some of the most delicate options to the right of the networks are non-terminal, so that the network cannot function as a fully explicitly generative device, and that Halliday fails to clarify what kind of unit might qualify as a point of origin for system networks, thus making the networks seem to imply a rankless semantics.
> (Fawcett, 1975: 32–36)

The systemic model places emphasis on meanings underlying linguistic forms; however, as Butler points out, Halliday's view on the relationship between syntax and semantics is never clearly stated. "The relationship between syntax and semantics is the subject of continuing controversy.... Halliday's main failing lies not so much in his refusal to recognize any clear borderline between syntax and semantics as in his reluctance to make clear the apparent shifts in his position" (Butler, 1985: 80–81).

Berry (1982) argues that, first, Halliday's theory remains just an outline of a theory, and there are few data in his discussion. Second, Halliday fails to define his terms adequately. Third, Halliday fails to clearly distinguish between facts and hypotheses. And, fourth, Halliday's shift away from syntagmatic relations toward paradigmatic relations has gone so far that syntagmatic phenomena have all but disappeared from his theories, so that his model cannot account for the total meaning potential.

In their *Reflections on Systemic-Functional Linguistics*, Zhu and Yan voice three pieces of criticism. First, owing to the sheer complexity of language, the size and the delicacy of networks for subsystems are not made clear, and it is hard to enumerate all the system networks of a language. Second, the static description of language systems cannot account for the dynamic operation of language. Third, Systemic Linguistics has not yet made notable contribution to human-computer interaction and artificial intelligence on the level of discourse, although it does help with the computer's generation of clauses (Zhu & Yan, 2001: 14–16).

2.1.9 Section summary

This section has reviewed the growth and development of Systemic Linguistics. Systemic Linguistics, developed by Halliday and his followers, is a theory in which language, or any part of a language, is represented as a resource for making meaning by choosing from a set of probabilities. The output is the realization of the features chosen in the network.

Systemic modeling of linguistic phenomena is particularly relevant to the topic of this study, and system networks are a powerful tool to represent the sophisticated choices involved in the system of person. Having at this point covered the theoretical aspects of Systemic Linguistics, this book will make a tentative effort in Chapter Three to account for the system of person using the notation of system networks.

2.2 Lexicogrammar

In SFL, language is analyzed in three strata: semantics, lexicogrammar and phonology. The term "lexicogrammar" represents a view of language that combines what are traditionally known as "structure" (or syntax, grammar, etc.) and "words" (or vocabulary, etc.).

2.2.1 SFL's stratification theory

Traditional school grammar books acknowledge the stratification of language in that they contain chapters about the pronunciation, vocabulary, syntax, etc. In SFL, a stratum is seen as "a subsystem of a particular order of symbolic abstraction in language" (Matthiessen & Halliday, 2009: 96). There are three strata of language, i.e. semantics, lexicogrammar and phonology/graphology, representing meaning, wording and sound/writing systems respectively. The term "stratum" is taken over from Stratificational Linguistics in place of an earlier term, "level," which is used in a variety of other senses.

The relationship between strata is one of realization; i.e. the selection of meaning (semantics) is realized by the selection of wording (lexicogrammar), which is in turn realized by the selection of the actual expression (phonology/graphology). This can be conveniently illustrated as in Figure 2.3.

According to Halliday (1975, 1996), infants' protolanguage consists of only two strata, namely the stratum of content and the stratum of expression, with no

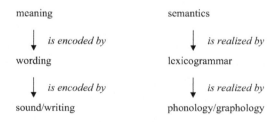

Figure 2.3 Stratification and realization

grammar in it yet. However, in adults' language, the content plane expands into two strata, lexicogrammar and semantics, which allows the meaning potential of human language to grow ad infinitum.

Systemicists maintain that language both construes human experience and enacts social relationships. The power of the semiotic process is largely vested in the act of meaning (see Halliday, 1992b). In the stratum of semantics, human experience and social processes are transformed into meaning; in the stratum of lexicogrammar, the meaning is in turn transformed into wording; in the stratum of phonology/graphology, the wording is further transformed into sound/writing.

The stratification of the content plane into lexicogrammar and semantics is said to have had profound significance in the evolution of human species, and "it is not an exaggeration to say that it turned *homo* . . . into *homo sapiens*. It opened up the power of language and in so doing created the modern human brain" (Halliday & Matthiessen, 2004: 25).

By virtue of stratification, the modeling of language can be extended further into the exterior of language itself since the stratum of semantics can stand as a realization of context. In this sense, semantics is recognized as an interfacing part connecting the language system with higher social semiosis. At the other end, a further stratification may likewise occur within the expression plane. For the biological resource of making sounds, a stratum of phonetics can be separated from the stratum of phonology, which functions as the organizing principle of the forms and structures of speech sounds (Figure 2.4).

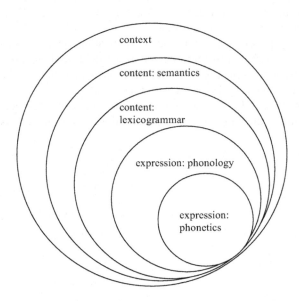

Figure 2.4 Extended stratification (Halliday & Matthiessen, 2004: 25)

2.2.2 Lexis as the most delicate grammar

2.2.2.1 Halliday's development of the lexicogrammatical model

As he investigates the relationship between lexis and grammar, Halliday observes that they are related systematically along the cline of delicacy, ordered from the most specific to the most general. In his influential paper "Categories of the Theory of Grammar" (1961), Halliday writes:

> The theoretical place of the move from grammar to lexis is . . . not a feature of rank but one of delicacy. . . . The grammarian's dream is . . . to turn the whole of linguistic form into grammar, hoping to show that lexis can be defined as "most delicate grammar."
>
> (Halliday, 1961: 267)

This notion, albeit speculative, expunges the strict demarcation between lexis and grammar and shows a departure from the traditionally accepted approach that views them as separate. However, in 1961 Halliday did not address the problem of lexical organization in terms of more delicate systems of grammatical modeling, since it was still the early stage of Scale and Category Grammar.

A more intense scrutiny of this "lexis as most delicate grammar" account was postponed until more than a decade later, when Halliday stated in a discussion with Herman Parret about "a social-functional approach to language" (Halliday, 1978: 36–58):

> The lexicon – if I may go back to a definition I used many years ago – is simply the most delicate grammar. In other words, there is only one network of lexicogrammatical options. And as these become more and more specific, they tend more and more to be realized by the choice of lexical item rather than by the choice of a grammatical structure. But it is still part of a single system.
>
> (Halliday, 1978: 43)

The term "lexicogrammar" refers to a unified linguistic resource of meaning potential in which lexis and grammar are distinguished in terms of generality and specificity. Halliday now sees the two linguistic forms of realization as one and not essentially different, with both being capable of conveying meanings that a language has to make available to its users.

2.2.2.2 Hasan's exploration of the "grammarian's dream"

Hasan (1987) is recognized as the first and most significant paper concentrating on discussions about Halliday's "grammarian's dream" of turning the entirety of linguistic form into grammar. Hasan explores the reality of that dream by examining two questions: (1) Is the project feasible? and (2) What would be the implications of that dream? By way of exemplification, she gives detailed examinations on the networks of three aspects of transitivity: the lexicogrammar of acquisition (the processes of *gather, collect* and *accumulate*), of deprivation 1 (*scatter, divide* and *distribute*) and of deprivation 2 (*stew, spill* and *share*).

While exploring the features that are associated with and unique to the nine lexical items, Hasan remarks that the uniqueness of features lies not simply in their individual identities as lexical items but also in their intralinguistic characteristics. Lexical items are idiosyncratic because each one entails a set of lexicogrammatical relationships with other linguistic forms. Thus, the features that determine lexical items can also be expressed by a set of realization statements.

On the basis of an in-depth account of the transitivity networks of the nine distinctive lexical items, though only the output of experiential metafunction, the conclusion is drawn that lexis is delicate grammar and the project of turning the whole of linguistic form into grammar is feasible.

As regards the second question, the implication of the "grammarian's dream" would be that "the ways in which the reference of *book* or *bag* is achieved [are] essentially the same as that for *is, in, on, that* and *the*" (Hasan, 1987: 208). And "the systemic functional view of an uninterrupted continuity between grammar and lexis . . . rejects the approach wherein the bricks of lexis are joined together by the mortar of grammar" (ibid.).

In accounting for the basis of the options of the networks and clarifying the value of features discovered in her study, Hasan holds that the "options of the networks are not 'universals', 'primitives' or god-given truths: they are schematic pointers to man-made meanings which can be expressed verbally. . . . The networks REPRESENT a language; they do not INVENT it" (Hasan, 1987: 207).

Therefore, the Systemic Grammar sets out to explore the feature options that lie at the heart of linguistic resources through expressing their meanings and relations with the systemic network notation.

2.2.3 Other systemicists' approaches to the lexis-grammar relation

2.2.3.1 M. Berry

Berry (1977) devises partial, tentative system networks for "Things" (nouns) and "Qualities" (adjectives/adverbs), representing the meaning distinctions which are carried by individual lexical items. This is considered an important attempt to adopt Halliday's notion of the "most delicate grammar" in the study of lexis. In her account, Berry attempts to draw a parallel between lexical and grammatical organization by comparing the collocations of lexical items to elements of grammatical structure. She even tries to postulate a "rank" for lexical organization as has been done for grammar; however, she has to admit that lexical senses are incompatible with the unit of the word on the assumed rank scale for grammatical description.

Between the notion of "lexis being subsumed under grammar" and the belief that "lexis will never be subsumed under grammar," Berry takes an intermediate position that acknowledges grammar and lexis as distinct yet related on a cline with no sharp division in between, differing only by degree. She also puts forward the possibility of combining the system networks and realization processes of grammar and lexis.

2.2.3.2 R. P. Fawcett

Fawcett (1980) treats lexis as the representation of the cultural classification of "Processes," "Things" and "Qualities," cultural classification being modeled as a more delicate part of relevant sub-networks. His model is designed to capture lexical specificity without overlooking grammatical generalization. In his own words, it "makes an appropriate connection between the syntactico-semantic generalizations associated with units such as the clause and the facts associated with given lexical items" (Fawcett, 1980: 271).

Fawcett (1980) provides examples of system networks of verbs and nouns. Verbs are accounted for in various networks of transitivity, with Processes classified into action, mental, etc. and further classified according to their association with participant roles. Nouns are probed into by the cultural classification of Things, with system networks specifying the semantic options based on taxonomic delicacies.

Fawcett's paper in 1987 offers an extensive treatment of the lexicogrammar of relational processes including three major types, i.e. locational, possessive and attributive processes. Comparable to Fawcett (1980, 1987), Hasan (1987) also seek to verify lexis' status as the most delicate grammar. What is more, Fawcett's system network approach also paves the way for his subsequent (and also current) work on Cardiff Grammar, a model of English grammar designed to be implemented computationally.

2.2.3.3 C.M.I.M. Matthiessen

Matthiessen's work on lexis focuses on the computerized generation of text, particularly lexical choices in text generation. Matthiessen (1990) explores a systemic approach to lexicogrammar, placing emphasis on the fact that the lexicogrammar realizes meanings from all three metafunctions. Along with grammar, lexis also takes into account the interpersonal and textual metafunctions rather than simply reflecting its ideational organization (Matthiessen, 1990: 259).

According to Matthiessen (1990: 267), interpersonal and textual lexis may either make independent contributions or combine with ideational lexis. Interpersonal lexis makes its independent contribution through modal expressions; textual lexis through phoric ones. Interpersonal lexis combines with ideational lexis in terms of connotation, and textual lexis combines with ideational lexis in terms of lexical cohesion.

In addition, Matthiessen also stresses the influence of context on lexical options, suggesting that the choice of lexically realized functions is influenced by situational factors. Field, tenor and mode exert an impact on the lexical choices within the ideational, interpersonal and textual metafunctions respectively.

2.2.3.4   G. H. Tucker

Tucker has been working together with Fawcett on the development of Cardiff Grammar, his particular concentration being the lexical aspects of the grammar. Tucker (1998) is known as the only book-length contribution to lexis within the systemic functional theory and has been hailed as "the most complete study ever made (in any theory of language) of 'qualities' in English (roughly, 'adjectives' and 'manner adverbs'), and their realization in the 'quality group'" (Fawcett, 2008: 4). Indeed, this work takes a unified approach to lexis and grammar in the study of adjectives, or, in other words, "a lexicogrammar of Quality" (Tucker, 1998: 8). The author specially stresses that "a systemic functional grammar of a language ... provides an account of the semantic potential from the point of view of how it is linguistically expressed" (ibid.).

Tucker (2005) explores the possibility of revising and extending the systemic lexicogrammatical framework to incorporate some phenomena in spoken discourse that exist awkwardly alongside the clause as the principal unit of lexicogrammatical organization, thus providing a more inclusive and integrated account of them.

Tucker (2007) addresses the challenge posed by phraseological phenomena to the conception of the language system as consisting of a set of general syntactic rules and principles and a separate lexicon. According to Tucker (2007), the challenge presented by phraseological phenomena is demonstrated in their apparent encompassment of aspects of both grammatical and lexical organization. "The decision to focus on grammar or lexis depends on the linguistic researcher's perspective, but ultimately they are complementary perspectives on the nature of linguistic expression" (Tucker, 2007: 954).

2.2.4   *Rejection of the lexis/grammar distinction by non-systemic functionalists*

Apart from the systemic functional approach to the description of language that prioritizes the lexicogrammar in terms of meaning potential, there are other linguistic schools and frameworks that reject the distinction between the lexicon and grammar, especially Construction Grammar, Head-Driven Phrase Structure Grammar, Cognitive Grammar and Lexical-Functional Grammar (Jackendoff, 2007: 53–54). The following briefly reviews the standpoint on eliminating the borderline between syntax (grammar) and lexis held by some cognitive linguists.

2.2.4.1   R. W. Langacker

While the distinction between grammar and the lexicon is regarded as important in the tradition of transformational grammar, and a given linguistic expression needs to be classified as either "in the syntax" or "in the lexicon," Langacker (1987) dismisses this as an insubstantial question. He argues that those transformational theorists who adopt this view simply lack an independent, fine-grained, empirically grounded appreciation of the lexical phenomena and thus are ignorant of the devices needed to deal with such problems. He further elaborates that

> [s]yntax was thought of as the domain of generality and regularity, of productive rules with fully predictable outputs; anything falling short of these standards was relegated to the purgatory of lexicon – the domain of irregularity, idiosyncrasy, and lists. But this deeply ingrained, almost archetypical conception of syntax has very little empirical foundation.
> (Langacker, 1987: 26)

Langacker does not believe that linguistic constructions can be neatly divided into two groups on the basis of generality, or that the regular aspects of language can be segregated from the irregular ones in any meaningful way. He seriously criticizes the practice of distinguishing between syntax and the lexicon in transformational grammar as "ill-defined"; additionally, with regard to the increasingly frequent exile of the so-called irregular constructions from the syntax into the lexicon, his repudiation is that "moving these phenomena from one box to another has singularly failed to illuminate them" (ibid.).

2.2.4.2 R. Jackendoff

As a generative and cognitive linguist, Jackendoff disapproves of the distinction between the lexicon and grammar as merely an assumption carried over from traditional grammar that roughly accords with common sense. In correcting what he calls "a fundamental mistake" of the lexicon/grammar distinction maintained by Chomsky's influential *Aspects of the Theory of Syntax* (1965), Jackendoff voices a viewpoint that somewhat resembles that of SFL:

> [A] word is best regarded as a type of interface rule that establishes a partial correspondence among pieces of phonological, syntactic, and semantic structure, such that each piece conforms to the formation rules of its own component. In other words, the language does not consist of a lexicon *plus* rules of grammar. Rather, lexical items are *among* the rules of grammar.
> (Jackendoff, 2007: 55)

Through exemplification of the problems brought about by idiomatic expressions in English, Jackendoff (2007) reaches the conclusion that linguistic expressions of all sizes stored in human memory, from individual morphemes to full idiomatic sentences, fall along a continuum of generality defined by the number and range of variables they contain. His idea of the continuum of generality is best epitomized as follows:

> At one extreme are wordlike constants.... Moving along the continuum, we find mixtures of idiosyncratic content and open syllables in idioms.... Still more general are the argument structures of individual predicates.... Finally,

at the other extreme are rulelike expressions consisting only of very general variables.... As a consequence, the formal distinction between lexical items and rules of grammar vanishes.

(Jackendoff, 2007: 58–59)

Thus, the difference between a word and a rule is broken down, and both are seen as pieces of structure that are stored in long-term memory.

2.2.5 Section summary

In opposition to the transformational linguistic school's treatment of the lexicon as a component of language distinct from the rules of grammar, a great number of linguists have argued for the dissolution of the lexis/grammar dichotomy. The unity of lexical items and grammatical rules represents a new and insightful perception that stimulates a rethinking of language organization. A study of the concept of person in terms of the complementarity between its lexical and grammatical expressions will follow in Chapter Four and Chapter Five.

2.3 Chapter summary

This chapter looks back on the evolution and existing contributions of the two theoretical frameworks that are most germane to the present study, i.e. Systemic Linguistics and lexicogrammar. The systemic theory and the idea of complementarity between lexis and grammar have respectively inspired many works on the description and interpretation of linguistic phenomena, as has been indicated in the above literature review. However, the concept of person has not attracted much attention within these two theoretical domains. Partial studies related to person are scattered here and there: Fawcett (1988) is the most representative instance of using systemic theory to account for person, but the scope of the study is confined to English personal pronouns; Siewierska (2004) dedicates the first section of the second chapter to the morpho-phonological person forms across languages, but the focus is by and large on grammatical realizations and the work is a non-SFL one.

Therefore, this book is intended to integrate systemic theory with the notion of lexis-grammar unity, so as to account systemically for the semantic features in the concept of person and reveal the complementarity between lexical and grammatical realizations of person forms.

3   Person as a system

This chapter is concerned with the semantics of person in the functioning of language. The seemingly simple and uncontroversial concept of person could be genuinely more complex than is generally taken for granted. The systemic description of the data as regards person, even when as apparent and straightforward as for English personal pronouns, involves a series of questions (see Fawcett, 1988). However, Fawcett (1988) does not deal with every aspect of English personal pronouns (e.g. reflexivity) and decides to exclude the category of case from the description, let alone account for the bigger picture of the manifestation of person in language. Therefore, this chapter will at first try to provide an account of the bigger picture related to person and then of how it fits into the semantic choice networking.

3.1   Person reinterpreted

In systemic functional practice, person is generally viewed as a subsystem of the system of MOOD; Halliday and Matthiessen (2004: 135) provide a system network of English mood, in which person is mingled with Subject, shown in Figure 3.1.

And then depending on the mood type the subject can be realized either implicitly or explicitly. This treatment of person is a problematic one in that it seems to be indicating that person only has to do with the choosing of the Subject in a clause. Actually, person can be reflected in the Finite element of the mood structure and Residue as well.

Looked at from the perspective of experiential meaning, a clause can be analyzed in terms of its transitivity structure, which is composed of Process, Participant and Circumstantial elements. It might sound fanciful and ungrounded to claim that the concept of person can be realized in all three transitivity elements; however, this study will prove that this claim is not an unaccountable whim but an observable and justifiable fact. The ubiquitous person frequents almost everywhere in language, both semantically and lexicogrammatically. This point will be further elaborated in the next chapter.

Having used the term "person" so many times, this book ought to offer a comprehensive account of the semantic nature of this linguistic concept. Here the notion of person is not confined to its manifestation in any specific language but

30 *Person as a system*

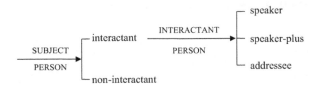

Figure 3.1 System network of SUBJECT: person (excerpted from Halliday & Matthiessen, 2004: 135)

is observed in general and interpreted in light of the universal human ability to construe experiences of events and exchanges.

Person forms, in essence, are expressions of identification of and reference to participant roles in discourse. These identifying and referential expressions, be they explicit or implicit, build up a relationship among the discourse initiator, the discourse recipient and any other party or parties in the context of situation. Various types of person forms in discourse function as access to the cognitive establishment or retrieval of participant information. In this sense, a discourse, either spoken or written, is viewed as "a hierarchically structured, mentally represented sequence of utterance and indexical acts which the participants are engaging in as the communication unfolds" (Cornish, 1999: 34).

An important term in Systemic Functional Linguistics that is very close to person is "tenor," which is one of the three components of the context of the situation, the other two being field and mode. The three contextual factors collectively constitute the register of a discourse. Halliday (1978) defines "tenor" as follows:

Tenor – the role structure

the cluster of socially meaningful participant relationships, both permanent attributes of the participants and role relationships that are specific to the situation, including the speech roles, those that come into being through the exchange of verbal meanings.

(Halliday, 1978: 142–143)

The term "tenor" is similar to the concept of person under discussion in the sense that both focus on participant roles and relationships in a discourse. However, this study adopts the term "person" as the subject of discussion since "tenor" is specifically restricted to being a metafunctional contextual variable in the analysis of register while "person" can be used in a broader range.

The concept of person can be realized through an extensive range of independent and dependent morpho-phonological forms, or even their absence, including proper names, demonstrative deictics, pronouns, clitics, affixes, inflections, etc. This book will come back to these various encoding devices and their association with the accessibility of participant roles and with the construal of experience in Chapter Four and Chapter Five.

There are, above all, several questions to be answered: How are person-related semantic choices made? How is person meaning realized lexicogrammatically in terms of systemic networking? What other systems does the system of person come across, necessarily or optionally, in its realization into lexicogrammar?

3.2 System networks of person

3.2.1 *Nominality vs. pronominality*

When a participant is to be manifested and identified in discourse, its realization usually requires the choice between a nominal form and a pronominal form. Consider Example 3.1:

> Example 3.1 An **economist** is an **expert who** will know tomorrow why the things **he** predicted yesterday didn't happen today.[1]

The core participant in the above piece of discourse is first mentioned as *economist*, which is a common noun, and then identified through a relational process as an *expert*, another common noun as the predicated object. At the third mention, this participant is referred to by means of a relative pronoun *who*, which introduces a relative clause and has the double role of referring back to the antecedent and functioning as the subject in the embedded clause. The fourth mention is realized by the personal pronoun *he*. The identity of the participant is recoverable through the phoricity system in language, which enables an important cohesive device, i.e. reference.

On this primary stage, a participant is introduced into the discourse or retrieved from it by means of either nominal or pronominal realization, depending on whether the participant is already in the immediate linguistic, situational or cognitive context or not. The nominal vs. pronominal distinction is essentially a semantic one. Either of the options makes a meaning of its own, and more options are to be encountered as the delicacy goes deeper. Again each option has its own idiosyncratic meaning.

Semantic choices via intersections with other subsystems such as DISCOURSE ROLE, NUMBER and CASE have not yet been involved, so for the moment the person forms under discussion are only third person, singular and nominative. The system network should be represented as in Figure 3.2.

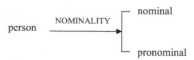

Figure 3.2 Subsystem of nominality vs. pronominality

32 *Person as a system*

Probed into further at a higher delicacy, pronominal forms can be subdivided into a number of heterogeneous types, including personal pronouns (e.g. *he, she, it*), demonstrative pronouns (e.g. *this, that*), reciprocal pronouns (e.g. *each other, one another*), relative pronouns (e.g. *who, which, that*), interrogative pronouns (e.g. *who, which*) and indefinite pronouns (e.g. *all, some, any, no*). Reflexive pronouns (e.g. *myself, themselves*) are left out for the moment and will be picked up in Section 3.2.7.

On the other hand, a nominal expression can be either a proper noun, like the name of an individual person, place or organization, or a common noun signifying a class of object or a concept. Again, as the delicacy grows deeper, there may be further choices between concrete and abstract nouns, or between count and non-count nouns. However, such delicacy is not required in the present study. What is more, the nominal form is not confined to a single noun but on most occasions is a nominal group, like *an economist* and *an expert* in the above example. The nominal group can be extended to the utmost, as in Table 3.1, using functional labels (with uppercase initials) established by Systemic Functional Grammar.

Admittedly, the concept of person sometimes does not rely solely on either nominal or pronominal forms, and sometimes neither of them may be present at all; for example, verb conjugations in some languages are equally capable of fulfilling the task. Or different ways work together to denote the idea of person. However, the other means of indicating person, such as conjugation and ellipsis, are not included in the system network, since they are not immediately relevant to the subject matter of the present subsection. These otherwise identifiable denotations of participant roles are given an open space in the system network of person with nominality as the current scope of study.

Thus, the system network can be further extended as shown in Figure 3.3.

Table 3.1 Elements of a nominal group

Deictic	Post-deictic	Numerative	Epithet	Classifier	Thing	Qualifier
the	other	three	comfortable	rocking	chairs	on sale

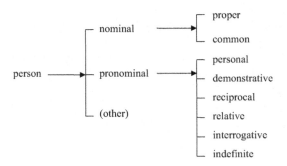

Figure 3.3 Subsystem of nominality vs. pronominality (extended)

It should be noted again that the term "person" here does not necessarily imply that it ought to be a human or animate participant; the term "person" is applicable to any participating entity in a discourse, including the inanimate or abstract, such as *the things* in Example 3.1 above.

3.2.2 Discourse role

As was briefly mentioned in Chapter One, person forms are fundamentally divided into the first and second person on the one hand and the third person on the other. This is due to the underlying difference in terms of discourse roles between the interactants in a discourse and the non-interactants. Martin (1992: 112) refers to them as "interlocutors" and "non-interlocutors." Use of the terms "participants" and "non-participants" in the sense of distinguishing the first/second person and the third person should be eschewed because, as suggested in this book, the third persons are also participants in a discourse, only they are not interacting parties but are brought into play by the addresser and/or addressee.

On this basis, it would not be surprising to learn that some languages, such as Salt-Yui, a Papuan language, do not have the grammatical person expressions for the third person, which can be realized only by lexical means (Irwin, 1974: 32), or that the third person pronouns originate from demonstrative deictics, as is demonstrated by the example of Latin at the very beginning of this book. In languages which have the full set of grammatical first, second and third person markers, there may exist a striking difference between the expressions for the first/second person and the third person. That is to say, the first and second person markers share some similarities in phonological, morphological or syntactic features, as opposed to the third person forms. For example, the third person singular personal pronouns in English include three types (*he, she, it*) in accordance with gender distinctions (masculine, feminine and neuter), whereas there is no such tripartite distinction for the first and second person pronouns. Example 3.2 is from the northern dialect of the Yi language, which is spoken by the Yi people in southwestern China's Sichuan and Yunnan provinces. The first and second singular personal pronouns are observed to exhibit a phonological proximity, in contrast to the third person form.

Example 3.2 Liangshan Yi language (Ding et al., 1991)

nga   1 SG
nə   2 SG
tshʅ   3 SG

The fundamental differences between the first and second person on the one hand and the third person on the other are usually attributed to the fact that the interpretation of the first and second persons depends heavily on the extralinguistic context of the discourse. The first and second person forms, especially their grammatical realizations, are essentially deictic. According to Jakobson (1971: 131), such grammatical units are referred to as "shifters" by Jespersen, and "their meaning cannot be defined without a reference to the message." In contrast,

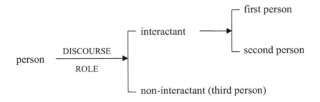

Figure 3.4 Subsystem of DISCOURSE ROLE

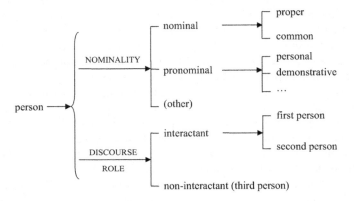

Figure 3.5 System of person featuring NOMINALITY and DISCOURSE ROLE

third person expressions are mostly either anaphoric grammatical forms or lexical units whose references are retrievable exophorically.

Thus, the system network of person reflecting semantic options among discourse roles would look as in Figure 3.4.

If this is combined with the subsystem network of nominality vs. pronominality, a system network of person with two intersecting semantic fields results at this stage, shown in Figure 3.5.

According to Figure 3.5, choices must be made simultaneously in terms of both nominality/pronominality and discourse role. The consequence is that any of the first, second and third persons may take the form of proper nouns, common nouns, personal pronouns, demonstratives or other expressions that are left open.

3.2.3 *Number*

Although research has revealed that the existence of number distinctions in person paradigms is not universal, absence of number marking in any person paradigm is highly exceptional (Corbett, 2000: 50–51). It is a rather safe assertion that there exists a palpable relationship between person and number. The requirement of concordance between the category of person and number often leads to the morpho-phonological agreement between the person form and certain finite verbs, such as the co-occurrence of *he* with *is* and *they* with *are* in English, or that of *je* with *vais* and *nous* with *allons* in French.

The number in person expressions can be signified in a number of ways. For nominal expressions, a number-indicating suffix can be attached, such as *pupil – pupils* in English and 学生-学生们 in Chinese; there is generally no explicit number indicator affiliated to inanimate nouns in Chinese. For personal pronouns, number is typically denoted by suppletive forms in European languages, e.g. *I* vs. *we* in English, *ich* vs. *wir* in German and *yo* vs. *nos* in Spanish, but by suffixation in some other languages, e.g. 我 vs. 我们 in Chinese and *watashi* vs. *watashitachi* in Japanese.

The simplest and most evident number opposition in the person paradigm is the singular-plural distinction. This distinction is based on the opposition between one and more than one entity. However, the term "plural" may have different implications in different languages. In languages such as Sanskrit where there is a dual number, "plural" means more than two. Even in languages with only the singular-plural distinction, "plural" might have a different meaning, too. According to Quirk et al. (1985: 297), "English makes the division after 'more than one' (e.g. *one half day, one day*), but *one and a half days, two days, one or two days*. . . ." This is unlike some languages where plural number indicates "two or more"; for example, in French, "one and a half days" is always *un jour et demi*.

3.2.3.1 Dual

Distinct from the singular and plural, the dual refers to two entities. When the semantic choice of duality is added to the system of person, this change gives "plural" a different meaning; that is, in a singular-dual-plural distinction, "plural" is used to denote three or more entities. In English, *both, either* and *neither* convey the sense of duality since they can only be used with reference to two, though *both* has plural concord and *either* and *neither* have singular concord (Quirk et al., 1985: 297). Example 3.3 provides a demonstration of the singular-dual-plural number system in Sanskrit.

Example 3.3 Singular-dual-plural number system in Sanskrit (Stenzler, 1915: 14, 26)

aśvaḥ	SG	NOM	"a horse"
aśvau	DU	NOM/ACC/VOC	"two horses"
aśvāḥ	PL	NOM/VOC	"(more than two) horses"
aham	SG	NOM	"I"
āvām	DU	NOM/ACC	"we two"
vayam	PL	NOM	"we (more than two)"

3.2.3.2 Trial

The trial number is for referring to three entities. The addition of trial into the number system will cause the system to possess four choices, namely singular, dual, trial and plural. Consequently, the meaning of "plural" will have to change again.

36 *Person as a system*

Such a system is found in some Indonesian, Malayo-Polynesian and Austronesian languages (see Corbett, 2000: 21–22). It is also interesting to know from Corbett (2000: 21) that the words "dual" and "trial" originate from the numerals "two" and "three," and that "plural" comes historically from "four."

3.2.3.3   Quadral, paucal and greater

Some rare languages of the Austronesian family have a separate set of forms for the quantity of four, i.e. the quadral number; some have expressions specifically for a small number of entities, i.e. paucal (similar to English "a few"); still others have a further distinction into exotically different types of plurality (Corbett, 2000: 22–38). However, these are genuinely unusual and would not make much more sense for the present study than the commonly seen number distinctions in the more widely known languages.

3.2.3.4   Number unspecified

It is noteworthy that in some languages it is not so obligatory to choose between singular and plural forms, or make a commitment to any other specific number. Consider Example 3.4:

Example 3.4   Non-number-specifying expression in Chinese

我	在动物园	看到	了	袋鼠。
I	in zoo	see	PAST	kangaroo.

"I saw a kangaroo/kangaroos in the zoo."

In the above example, number is not specified by the nominal expression 袋鼠, which can be either singular or plural. The interpretation of number needs to rely on knowledge about the situation such as a shared experience with the speaker, or on further inquiry. Typological studies show that some languages have morphological distinctions among singular, plural and unspecified number, while in some other languages the general non-number-specifying meaning shares the form of either the singular or plural expression. This non-number-specifying "number" (if still called so) has been given various names, including "common number" (Jespersen, 1924), "unit reference" (Hayward, 1979), "transnumeral" (Biermann, 1982) and "general" (Andrzejewski, 1960; Corbett, 2000).

The network representing the choices of number in the system of person is shown in Figure 3.6.

3.2.4   Inclusiveness

A subsystem that is closely related to the number distinction in the system of person is inclusiveness. There is often an inclusive/exclusive opposition when more than one person is involved in the pronominal expressions of the first and second person. Such expressions demand a different interpretation from that of nouns.

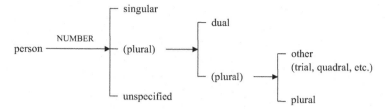

Figure 3.6 Subsystem of NUMBER

For example, the English first person plural *we* (and also the Chinese equivalent 我们) may refer to (a) the speaker plus the listener, (b) the speaker plus a third party, (c) the speaker plus the listener plus a third party, or (d) a group of simultaneous speakers in some special circumstances such as oath-taking or celebration.

Example 3.5 Various degrees of inclusiveness of *we*

(a) This is between you and me; **we** should never tell it to anybody else.
(b) My husband and I went camping last weekend. **We** had great fun!
(c) If you and Steve join us, **we**'ll be the strongest team ever.
(d) **We** are the champions. . . (sung by a winning soccer team)

The inclusive/exclusive dividing line in the first stage is between (a) and (c) on the one hand and (b) and (d) on the other hand, according to whether the addressee is included by the first person plural form. Some languages make a formal distinction between them, though English does not. Apalai, an Amazonian language spoken in the northern regions of Brazil, has such a morphological distinction.

Example 3.6 Apalai (Koehn & Koehn, 1986: 106)

(a) s-ynyh-ne
    INCL-sleep-IMP
    "Let's sleep."
(b) ynan-eneh-xi
    EXCL-bring it-IMP
    "Let us (exclusive) bring it."

The second person plural forms, such as *you* (*your*, *yourselves*) in English, are also likely to be interpreted in two different ways, according to whether a third party is included. The sentences in Example 3.7 show this difference.

Example 3.7 Third party inclusiveness/exclusiveness of second person plural

(a) You and your sister need to look after **yourselves** when Mum's not home.
(b) Thank **you** very much, ladies and gentlemen.

38 *Person as a system*

Table 3.2 Possible groups of participants (Cysouw, 2003: 74)

Group	Description
1+1	"we," mass speaking
1+2	"we," including addressee, excluding other
1+3	"we," including other, excluding addressee
2+2	"you-all," only present audience
2+3	"you-all," addressee(s) and others
3+3	"they"
1+2+3	"we," complete

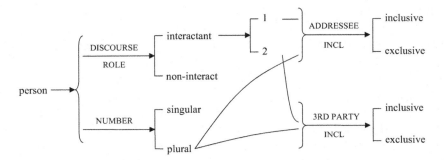

Figure 3.7 Subsystem of INCLUSIVENESS

Thus, the identifying possibilities of more than one participant in a discourse can be summed up by using the table from Cysouw (2003: 74).

The above seven distinctions of more than one person do not necessarily make a separate linguistic category each. Recent reports (Cysouw, 2003; Siewierska, 2004) suggest that the grammaticalized category for the 1+1 type has not yet been found in any known language in the world by distinguishing a particular morphological representation for group speech. Nor is the distinction between 2+2 and 2+3 linguistically salient. It is observed that in most major languages, the plural (in the sense of "more than one") pronominal markers of person stop at the delicacy of distinguishing singularity from plurality and do not proceed to tell inclusiveness and exclusiveness apart. This latter task can be accomplished only by nominal expressions. However, it is still worthwhile to include at least the basic inclusive/exclusive distinction (addressee inclusive vs. exclusive for first person plural; third party inclusive vs. exclusive for second person plural) in the system network due to its reflection of difference on the semantic level. And the system network of INCLUSIVENESS is necessarily represented in conjunction with those of DISCOURSE ROLE and NUMBER (Figure 3.7).

Of course, the system network can be extended if further distinction of plurality is incorporated into the analysis, as in Figure 3.8.

Person as a system 39

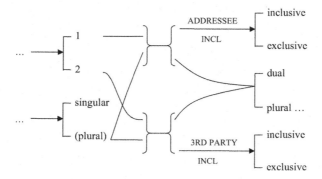

Figure 3.8 Subsystem of INCLUSIVENESS (extended to incorporate plurality)

3.2.5 *Gender*

Gender is another important system that intersects with the system of person. Hockett (1958: 531) defines gender as "classes of nouns reflected in the behavior of associated words." Corbett (2006) follows this definition. In fact, the category of gender evidently involves pronominals as well as nominals.

Gender distinctions are essentially based on the biological sex of the discourse participant: person forms identifying males are masculine, those for females feminine. There can also be another set of neuter forms. This distinction is seen, for instance, in the English third person singular pronouns *he, she* and *it*. Apart from the biological sex, the distinction of genders may also be predicated on other semantically motivated principles. This is commonly referred to as "grammatical gender," as in shown in Example 3.8.

Example 3.8 Grammatical genders in German

der Wagen	M	"the car"
die Hausaufgabe	F	"the homework"
das Buch	N	"the book"

Actually the term "gender" derives from the Latin word *genus* via Old French *gendre*, originally meaning "kind" or "sort," so it is not much surprising that the notion of gender transcends the biological sex. The tripartite distinction of gender is found in many Indo-European languages, such as German and Russian; however, some languages have only a two-way division, such as French (masculine and feminine) and Swedish (common gender and neuter gender). Some languages may have more than three grammatical genders. For example, Czech has four: animate masculine, inanimate masculine, feminine and neuter; and Polish has five: personal masculine, animate masculine, inanimate masculine, feminine and neuter. Here the gender system also combines with other systems like personhood and animacy.

Table 3.3 Gender-related phonological/orthographical saliency

Language	Example		Phonologically different	Orthographically different
Latin	*multus*	"many, much" M	Yes	Yes
	multa	"many, much" F		
	multum	"many, much" N		
French	*grand*	"big" M	Yes	Yes
	grande	"big" F		
	vrai	"true" M	No	Yes
	vraie	"true" F		
Chinese*	他	"he"	No	Yes
	她	"she"		
	它	"it"		

*The orthographic distinction among 他, 她 and 它 in modern Chinese did not start until 1917, under the influence of Western grammar. And the neuter 它 used to have two variants: 牠 for [+ANIMATE], 它 for [−ANIMATE] (Wang, 1980: 274).

In many of the gender-pervasive languages this grammatical feature requires concordance between the person forms and other morphological characteristics. Example 3.8 has already shown the agreement between nouns and their preceding definite articles.

According to a comprehensive report on gender by Corbett (1991), in some languages gender is central, while in some others it is entirely absent. And there are also various degrees of phonological and orthographical distinction of gender across languages. See Table 3.3 for a comparison.

3.2.5.1 Gender, number and discourse role

It is reported that the relationship between gender and discourse role is often expressed in the form of a typological hierarchy; i.e. "language should have gender either in the third person only, . . . or in the second and third persons only, . . . or in all three persons" (Siewierska, 2004: 105). For English personal pronouns in the nominative case, the system network incorporating GENDER, NUMBER and DISCOURSE ROLE is as follows:

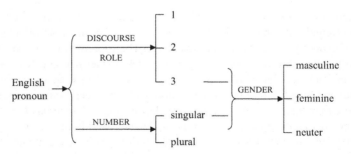

Figure 3.9 System network of English pronouns in the nominative case (after Fawcett, 1988)

Person as a system 41

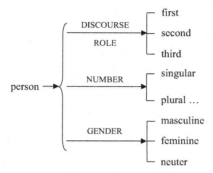

Figure 3.10 System of person featuring DISCOURSE ROLE, NUMBER and GENDER

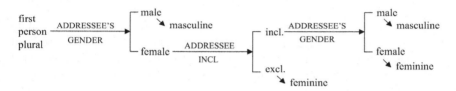

Figure 3.11 System of first person plural featuring GENDER and INCLUSIVENESS

However, if the semantic probabilities without specific language boundaries or restriction to pronouns are represented, the system network can be simplified to one with multiple entries. Networks for specific languages may derive from the general framework with proper modifications.

3.2.5.2 *Gender and inclusiveness*

It is interesting to note that gender may also interact with inclusiveness in person forms. There are languages, such as Spanish (*nosotros* M vs. *nosotras* F), that have a masculine vs. feminine gender distinction in the first person plural pronoun. And only when every member of a group is female is the feminine plural form used; otherwise, the masculine form is used. (This indeed works in many languages for the third person plural.) On such premises, when a female speaker is talking to a male listener and any third party involved is also female, the gender of the first person plural form she uses really depends on whether the addressee is included or not. If he is included, the "we" should be masculine; if not, feminine. It would not matter if the addressee is also a female, or when a male speaker is talking to either sex.

Thus, the system network for this occasion would be as in Figure 3.11. The system network for the second person plural for gender interacting with the inclusion/exclusion of a third party can be likewise devised.

3.2.6 Case

Person expressions in discourse may adopt morphological case markings to perform certain syntactic functions. Case, according to the definition by Blake (2001: 1), is "a system of marking dependent nouns for the type of relationship they bear to their heads." Blake continues to elaborate on the term "heads" by stating:

> Traditionally the term [case] refers to inflectional marking, and, typically, case marks the relationship of a noun to a verb at the clause level or of a noun to a preposition, postposition or another noun at the phrase level.
>
> (Blake, 2001: 1)

However, this definition seems to be indicating that case is a grammatical feature only of nouns. As a matter of fact, case marking applies to both nominal and pronominal forms, which is precisely relevant to the subject of study of this book. In addition, case marking may also be manifested on adjectives and numerals, which fall out of the scope of this study.

Some languages boast highly intricate case systems, and they are commonly referred to as case languages. For example, Latin adopts sophisticated inflectional case markings to show the syntactic relationships between a nominal/pronominal and the verb or preposition. An illustration is given in Example 3.9. The grammatical relation between a noun and the finite verb *dedit* is entirely determined by the case marking ending of each noun.

Example 3.9 Cases in Latin

Dominus   servō   pecūniam   dedit.
master-NOM slave-DAT   money-ACC   give-3 SG PERF
"The master gave (has given) the money to the slave."

Table 3.4 provides a case paradigm for the Latin noun *servus*.

It should be noted in passing that the masculine noun *servus* belongs to the second declension type in Latin, and there are four other types of nouns that require different paradigms of case marking. Therefore, it can be observed that the CASE

Table 3.4 Case paradigm of the Latin noun *servu*s

	SG	PL
NOM	serv**us**	serv**ī**
GEN	serv**ī**	serv**ōrum**
DAT	serv**ō**	serv**īs**
ACC	serv**um**	serv**ōs**
ABL	serv**ō**	serv**īs**
VOC	serv**e**	serv**ī**

Person as a system 43

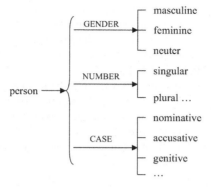

Figure 3.12 System of person featuring interaction of GENDER, NUMBER and CASE

system more often than not interacts with the type of the nominal/pronominal (typically determined by gender) and the NUMBER. To catch the gist of this interaction, a system network may be devised as shown in Figure 3.12.

It is easily seen from the system network that the person form at this stage is essentially dependent on a three-dimensional set of choices. The complexity of case marking and its intersection with gender and case make some case languages extremely difficult to learn for non-case language speakers. German has three genders, two numbers and four cases; Latin has three genders (but five noun types), two numbers and six cases; Sanskrit has three genders (but many more noun types depending on the ending), three numbers and eight cases; some other languages like Finnish and Hungarian have even more!

Not all languages have such convoluted case systems; instead, some mainly resort to word order as an alternative in distinguishing different syntactic relations. Modern English and Chinese adopt an SVO model as the unmarked clause type. And the word order of both can distinguish the direct object (accusative) from the indirect object (dative) in ditransitive structures, where the indirect object (Recipient) precedes the direct object (Goal). Interestingly, however, it works the other way round in some Chinese dialects such as Cantonese.

Example 3.10 Syntactic relations indicated by word order

(a) He   gave   **me**   **a book**.
    NOM   DAT   ACC
(b) 他   给 了   我   一本书。
    he-NOM   give PAST   me-DAT   a book-ACC
"He gave me a book."
(c) 佢   畀 咗   **本書**   **我**。
    he-NOM   give PAST   a book-ACC   me-DAT
"He gave me a book."

44 *Person as a system*

The second strategy to indicate syntactic relations is by means of prepositions or other "relators." For instance, in English, the dative case can be denoted by prepositions like *to* and *for* besides being conveyed by word order as mentioned above; the ablative case by *from* or *with*; the locative by *in, on, at*, etc.; and the genitive by *of* or *'s* attached to a noun. For Chinese, it is suggested that "relator nouns are a feature" (Blake, 2001: 16).

Instead of using inflectional suffixes, some languages attach particles to the participants of a clause without changing the nominal/pronominal per se to indicate case relations, such as Korean and Japanese, which are classified as agglutinative languages. (The *watashi ni* part in Example 3.11(b) is actually redundant, the reason for which will be clarified in the next chapter, where person-indicating verbs in Japanese are discussed.)

Example 3.11 Case relations indicated by particles in Korean and Japanese

(a) Geu **ga**   na **ege/hante**   chaek **eul**   jueossda.
    He NOM   I DAT   book ACC   give-PAST
    "He gave me a book."

(b) Kare **ga**   watashi **ni**   hon **wo**   kureta.
    He NOM   I DAT   book ACC   give-PAST
    "He gave me a book."

According to Siewierska (2004: 49), "it is often stated that morphological marking of core syntactic functions is more common with independent person forms than with lexical NPs." This is indeed so in the case of English pronouns. The case-signifying morphological contrast between *I* and *me*, and between *he* and *him*, is not seen in nouns, except that the genitive marker *'s* is retained.

Speaking of the genitive marker, there emerges the issue of what is often called the "possessive." There are generally two sets of possessives: one set functions syntactically as determiners, such as *my, your*, etc. in English; the other set is more noun-like, such as *mine, yours*, etc. The categorization of these genitive forms of personal pronouns remains highly inconsistent across languages. Table 3.5 shows how they are classified in English, French, Spanish and Italian respectively. The examples are all equivalent to the English *my* and *mine*, except that the other languages have distinctions in gender and number.

The difference in nomenclature does not in any sense distinguish the functions of these person forms. Therefore, it would be quite convenient to refer to them simply as personal pronouns in the genitive case or genitive personal pronouns.

3.2.7 *Reflexivity*

Reflexive person forms, as the term implies, reflect another nominal or pronominal element of the discourse. The reflexive and the reflected entities are in a co-referential relationship, as in *She bought herself a present.*

Table 3.5 Classification of genitive personal pronouns

English (Quirk et al., 1985)	determinative possessive pronoun	*my* . . .
	independent possessive pronoun	*mine* . . .
French (Price, 1993)	possessive determiner	*mon/ma/mes* . . .
	possessive pronoun	*le mien, la mienne, les miens, les miennes* . . .
Spanish (Bosque & Demonte, 1999)	prepositive possessive*	*mi, mis* . . .
	postpositive possessive*	*el mío, la mía, los míos, las mías* . . .
Italian (Proudfoot & Cardo, 1997)	possessive adjective	*il mio, la mia, i miei, le mie* . . .
	possessive pronoun	*il mio, la mia, i miei, le mie* . . .

* The terms are translated literally from *posesivo antepuesto* and *posesivo pospuesto* in Spanish.

Reflexive personal pronouns in English are formed through attachment of suffixes (*-self* for singular and *-selves* for plural). For the first and second person, the suffixes are added to genitive personal pronouns (*myself, yourself, ourselves, yourselves*), while for the third person, they are added to the accusative forms (*himself, herself, itself, themselves*). This readily serves as another piece of evidence for the fundamental distinction between the first and second person on the one hand and the third person on the other in terms of morphological features, a point that has been discussed in Section 3.2.2.

Some other languages, like French and Spanish, rely on clitics to denote the sense of reflexivity. Example 3.12 provides examples of French.

Example 3.12 Reflexivity in French

(a) Il **se** lave.
 he 3 REFL wash-3 SG PRES
 "He washes himself."
(b) Il est fier de **lui**.
 he be-3 SG PRES proud of 3 SG M REFL
 "He is proud of himself."
(c) Il ne pense qu'à **lui-même**.
 he only think of-3 SG PRES 3 SG M REFL EMPH
 "He only thinks of himself."

Out of the three sample clauses, only the emphatic reflexive operator *-même* is somewhat equivalent to the English *-self*; the other forms are different clitics adopted to express reflexivity, and they are commonly classified as special variants of personal pronouns. Some of them may also function as reciprocal clitics which indicate that the participants are acting on one another, as in:

Example 3.13 Reciprocal clitic in French

Nous   **nous**   comprenons.
we   1 PL RECP   understand-1 PL PRES
"We understand each other."

In this example the second *nous* belongs to a different grammatical category and functions differently from the first one.

In Chinese, the reflexive pronoun is 自己, which means "self" and can be attached to either personal pronouns or nouns, or even stand by itself with or without an explicit referent in the co-text.

Example 3.14 Reflexive pronoun 自己 in Chinese

(a) 他要战胜的   正是   他   自己。
    the one he needs to defeat be-EMPH   he   REFL
    "He needs to defeat nobody but himself."
(b) 这些简单的事情   应该   让孩子们   自己   做。
    Such simple things should   make the children REFL   do
    "The children should be made to do such simple things themselves."
(c) 她   总   担心   别人   不   喜欢   自己。
    she   always   worry   others   NEG   like   REFL
    "She always worries that others don't like her (?herself)."
(d) 自己的   事情   自己   做。
    REFL GEN   thing   REFL   do
    "Do one's own thing by oneself."

Moreover, the Chinese reflexive pronoun does not have to agree in gender or number as it does in many European languages, including English.

If REFLEXIVITY is integrated into the system network of person as another probable option, it will be most convenient for reflexive pronouns, either independent or clitic, to be counted as a separate type of pronominal, parallel to personal pronouns, relative pronouns, demonstrative pronouns, etc. The system network for that part is given in Figure 3.13.

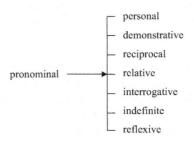

Figure 3.13 Extended classification of pronominals

If reflexive pronouns in English are the sole subject of study, Figure 3.9 can be applied as well with the entry condition changed to reflexives. The features of English reflexive pronouns are case-neutral and dependent only on the discourse role and number, hence the correspondence with Figure 3.9.

3.2.8 Emphasis

The suffix *-self* in English discussed in the previous subsection not only conveys reflexivity but also concerns emphasis on some occasions, as exemplified by Example 3.15(a). What is meant by emphasis is actually prominence of the person information in discourse; it generates the meaning of contrast or intensification. In English there are other intensifying expressions (mostly adjuncts) that emphasize the person forms as illustrated by (b)–(g) below.

Example 3.15 Emphatic person forms in English

(a) I **myself** cooked the meal.
(b) The new arrival was **none other than** the president.
(c) **Even** a child can answer this question.
(d) You are **the very** person I've been looking for.
(e) What happened to **your own** car? I can't lend you mine.
(f) Time **alone** will show who is right.
(g) Julie is **the only** woman for the job.

Salience of person forms in discourse not only can be expressed by emphatic person markers, as shown above, but can also be achieved by prosodic (such as stress, pitch and intonation), morphological (such as affixes, clitics and particles) and syntactic means (such as special word order and cleft or pseudo-cleft structures).

However, not all languages need to resort to such means to realize emphasis of person forms. In some languages, like Spanish and Italian, explicit use of personal pronouns is seen to be emphatic enough. See an example from Spanish in Example 3.16.

Example 3.16 Emphasis realized by explicit use of personal pronoun

(a) Soy   viejo.
 be-1 SG PRES old-M SG
 "I am old."
(b) **Yo** soy   viejo.
 I   be-1 SG PRES old-M SG
 "I (emphatic) am old."

There does exist a first person singular pronoun, *yo*, in Spanish, but it does not have to be there in a clause because the discourse role remains intact via the conjugation of the verb. When *yo* appears in (b), it indicates a sense of emphasis or contrast. It is I who am old, not anybody else.

48 *Person as a system*

Or a separate set of pronouns can be designated as having emphatic meaning. Recall (b) and (c) in Example 3.12. The reflexive form *lui* (or with an intensifier *-même*) belongs to another set of pronouns in French which are called "disjunctive pronouns" (Price, 1993: 134). They are distinct from the unmarked "conjunctive" ones in that they carry a series of special functions. One of these functions is emphasis. Compare the emphatic *toi* and *lui* with the unemphatic *tu* and *le* (contracted as *l'*) in the following examples.

Example 3.17 Emphatic personal pronoun in French

(a) **Toi,**   **tu**   ne peux pas venir.
    you-EMPH   you-NOM   can't come.
    "*You* can't come."

(b) **Lui,**   je   l'   aime beaucoup.
    him-EMPH   I   him-ACC   like very much.
    "I like *him* very much."

In a nutshell, when it comes to a person expression, whether it is emphatic or not should also be taken into account at the entry point of the system of person (Figure 3.14). Different languages may have different resources to implement the emphatic meaning; a system network for emphatic person forms in English is provided in Figure 3.15.

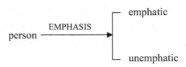

Figure 3.14 Subsystem of EMPHASIS

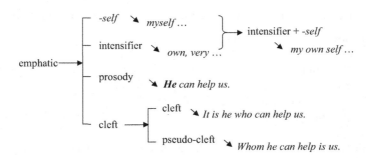

Figure 3.15 Emphatic person forms in English

3.2.9 Honorification

In the system of person, special person forms called honorifics are sometimes used to express social relations which are closely associated with social status, rank or class. Lexical encoding of honorific social deixis may cover a wide range of probabilities, such as the use of titles, surnames, kinship terms, euphemisms, etc. Grammatically, social distance and respect can be signaled by different modalities: the choice of honorific personal pronouns, auxiliaries, number distinction and suffixation, to name a few.

Although they may be found occasionally for the first and the third person, honorific person forms are typically spotted for the second person. For example, in modern Japanese, there are three commonly used second person singular pronouns, namely *anata*, *kimi* and *omae*. Among them, *anata* is considered the most distant and respectful, *omae* the most intimate and casual, while *kimi* is somewhere in the middle. Therefore, it would indeed be strange for someone to address his/her close friend using *anata*, or to address someone he/she is not so well acquainted with using *kimi* or *omae*. However, the appropriate use of address terms by Japanese on various occasions and to various addressees is far more complicated than simply distinguishing the three special second person terms. It depends on a variety of social parameters such as age, gender and the social standing of the interactants. The actual realization of honorific forms may accordingly vary along an extensive lexicogrammatical cline including nominal address forms, proper verb choices, personal pronouns and a series of grammatical honorific affixes and markers.

Apart from use of the more readily noticeable lexical means, the semantic feature of honorification can be encoded or realized grammatically via number distinction. This is suggested by Head (1978) as the most widely employed semantic distinction for the purpose of respect. In many languages the second person plural form is used to indicate deference and distance in referring to a single addressee. The technical term for this – "T/V distinction" – comes from French, where the second person plural *vous* rather than the singular *tu* is adopted to convey social distance or respect. Before the Norman Conquest, *thou* was the second person singular pronoun in English and *you* the plural. After the Frenchmen's conquest, *you* was gradually adopted for polite reference to a single addressee until finally *thou* disappeared altogether from daily use of English. Brown and Levinson (1987: 198–199) suggest a number of possible motives for this phenomenon. One is that "'you' (plural) provides a conventional 'out' for the hearer. . . . [I]t does not *literally* single out the addressee, it is *as if* the speaker were giving [the addressee] the option to interpret it as applying to him"; the other possible motive is "to treat persons as representatives of a group rather than as relatively powerless individuals."

A second frequently found practice of indicating respect is the variation of discourse role. The use of third person forms for the second person is usually adopted as an indication of lack of familiarity between the interactants, and of formality or deference toward the addressee. This phenomenon can be seen in languages like Spanish and Italian. In Spanish, the singular and plural honorific "you" (*usted* and *ustedes*) have third person concord; i.e. they agree with the third person singular

Table 3.6 German personal pronoun paradigm

	SG					PL			2 HON SG&PL
	1	2	3			1	2	3	
			M	F	N				
NOM	ich	du	er	**sie**	es	wir	ihr	**sie**	**Sie**
GEN	meiner	deiner	seiner	**ihrer**	seiner	unser	euer	**ihrer**	**Ihrer**
DAT	mir	dir	ihm	ihr	ihm	uns	euch	**ihnen**	**Ihnen**
ACC	mich	dich	ihn	sie	es	uns	euch	**sie**	**Sie**

and plural conjugations respectively. In Italian, the second person honorific pronoun shares the same form as the third person feminine form, only with an uppercase initial, i.e. *lei* (she) vs. *Lei* (you SG HON); *loro* (they) vs. *Loro* (you PL HON). All the honorific second person forms have third person concord. See Example 3.18.

Example 3.18 Second person honorific with third person form

(a) ¿**Tiene**   **usted**   mi libro?
    have-3 SG   you-HON   my book
    "Do you have my book?"

(b) Mi auguro   che   **faccia**   un buon viaggio.
    I hope   that   make-3 SG   a nice journey.
    "I hope that you'll have a nice journey."

Interestingly, in German, the honorific second pronoun paradigm incorporates all three features: plurality, third person and femininity, as is shown in Table 3.6.

In Korean and Japanese, honorific suffixes may be attached to a person's name or title, e.g. *-sama, -san, -kun* (Japanese) and *-nim, -ssi, -gun, -hyeong* (Korean). They function to transform plain appellations into honorific ones.

It is reported by Siewierska (2004: 224) that reflexive forms in some languages can also be associated with honorification. Thus, a system network for honorific usage of person forms can be devised as in Figure 3.16.

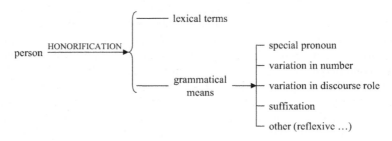

Figure 3.16 Subsystem of HONORIFICATION

More interestingly, honorific forms of second and third person pronouns in Chinese can be indicated by a phonological addition /n/ to the less formal forms *nĭ* and *tā* respectively, hence the honorifics *nín* and *tān*, except that the second person changes to a rising tone. Orthographically, the radical of "heart" (心) is attached to the informal pronoun to make it more respectful and cordial, as in 您 vs. 你 and 怹 vs. 他. However, the third person honorific pronoun has virtually gone out of use in modern Mandarin Chinese.

3.2.10 Proximity

The notion of proximity is particularly relevant to demonstratives. It has been pointed out in the first chapter that in many languages, such as Latin, the third person pronouns originate from demonstratives. In English, referential demonstratives *this, that, these* and *those* are gender-neutral but distinctive in proximity, number and modifierhood. Halliday and Hasan (1976) presents the three systematic distinctions as follows:

(1) between "near" (*this, these*) and "not near" (*that, those*)
(2) between "singular" (*this, that*) and "plural" (*these, those*)
(3) between Modifier (*this*, etc, plus noun, eg: *this tree is an oak*) and Head (*this*, etc, without noun, eg: *this is an oak*).

(Halliday & Hasan, 1976: 60)

The system network is represented in Figure 3.17, with the wh-interrogative *which* also taken into account.

The choice between "modifier" and "head" actually does not affect the form at all. Their function of endophoric reference and their relevance to cohesion are addressed at length by Halliday and Hasan (1976: 59–70). In Chinese, the demonstratives 这, 那, 这些, 那些, 哪 follow a similar paradigm as their English counterparts, except that there is a separate plural interrogative demonstrative 哪些 in Chinese.

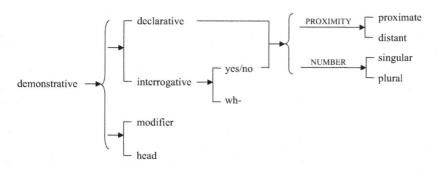

Figure 3.17 Referential demonstratives in English

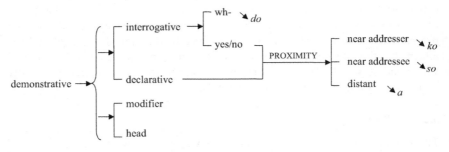

Figure 3.18 Referential demonstratives in Japanese

Referential demonstratives in Japanese present a different picture. Instead of the two-way distinction in proximity, the Japanese language distinguishes three categories: those demonstratives beginning with *ko* indicate nearness to the speaker; those beginning with *so* nearness to the listener; and those beginning with *a* denote distance from both the speaker and the listener. Bringing in the wh-interrogative demonstratives that begin with *do*, the paradigm is commonly referred to as *ko-so-a-do* groups of words. Unlike English, where *this*/*these* and *that*/*those* can either stand alone as a pronoun or head or precede a nominal expression as a determiner or modifier, the *ko-so-a-do* groups in Japanese adopt different forms with or without a following nominal. Compare (a) and (b) in Example 3.19.

Example 3.19 *ko* demonstratives in Japanese

(a) **Kore** wa   nan   desu ka.
    this TOP   what   be INT
    "What's this?"

(b) **Kono**   kotoba no   imi wa   nan   desu ka.
    this   word GEN   meaning TOP   what   be INT
    "What's the meaning of this word?"

As for number, although a plural suffix *ra* can be attached to the independent demonstratives, e.g. *korera* (these), *sorera* (those), it is not obligatory. The uninflected forms can be used as either singular or plural. The system network should look like Figure 3.18.

The demonstratives in use are mostly third person markers. However, in some languages like Japanese and Korean, demonstratives can be regularly used to indicate the first and second person. In English, the demonstratives *this* and *that* can refer to the first and second person in particular situations, such as a telephone conversation.

3.2.11 Other subsystems

Apart from the subsystems for the realization of a person form to go through that are outlined above, there might be other points of choice, i.e. subsystems that the system of person interacts with, which it is impossible for this book to exhaust owing to the enormous variety in terms of the functioning of the world's languages. Sections 3.2.1–3.2.10 have provided the major and most prominent ones, and a few more are to be added in passing in this subsection before this chapter is concluded.

3.2.11.1 Topicality

The person forms in some languages may be controlled by their status in the information structure of the discourse. Examined from the perspective of textual metafunction, the topic is typically Given information, which is recoverable from the context, and it usually occupies the position of a Theme. Example 3.20 provides examples from Japanese and Korean, where the topical person form is indicated by topic marker *wa* and *neun/eun*[2] respectively.

Example 3.20 Topical person forms in Japanese and Korean

(a) **Watashi wa**   Roshiyago ga   dekinai.
    I TOP   Russian NOM   cannot do
    "I can't speak Russian."

(b) **Na neun**   hakkyo reul   kassta.
    I TOP   school ACC   go-PAST
    "I went to school."

In Tagalog, a major Philippine language where a clause naturally begins with the verb, the topic marker *ang* determines topicality and at the same time requires agreement with an affix on the verb. Note how the agreement prefixes on the verb vary with the change of topic.

Example 3.21 Topical person form in Tagalog (Martin, 1996: 230–231)

(a) **Na**-halata   ng babae   **ang boyfriend niya**   sa kalsada.
    AGR-noticed   PAR woman   TOP boyfriend her   CIRC street
    "The woman noticed her boyfriend in the street."

(b) **Naka**-halata   **ang babae** ng boyfriend niya   sa kalsada.
    AGR-noticed   TOP woman   PAR boyfriend her   CIRC street
    "The woman noticed a boyfriend of hers[3] in the street."

3.2.11.2 Polarity

Love (2000: 17) observes that in the northwestern Australian language Worora there is a separate set of personal pronouns used in negative clauses, such as *'kaui* (third person singular masculine negative) as opposed to *'indja* (third person singular masculine positive).

3.2.11.3 Tense/aspect

Siewierska (2004: 38) reports that person forms can be combined with tense/aspect in Africa's Mande language and Chadic languages as well as in a number of Austronesian languages, which has resulted from the fusion of a subject person marker and a following auxiliary verb.

3.2.11.4 Mood

Some languages in the northwestern American Pacific region are reported by Jacobsen (1979) as marking tense, aspect and mood in the person forms. That is, the person forms would be different across different mood types such as indicative or interrogative.

3.2.11.5 Definiteness

This choice works mainly with nominals, especially common nouns, and is usually indicated by definite or indefinite determiners. Personal pronouns are generally taken as definite in that they typically do not co-occur with the determiners; however, things are just not that simple. A section in the next chapter will come back to this subject.

3.3 Chapter summary

In this chapter, the core function of person as identifying and referring to the participant roles in the discourse has been discussed. Far from being merely a subsystem in the Mood structure that makes a distinction among the first, second and third person participant roles, the system of person covers a wide range of semantic fields and necessarily interacts with a good number of other subsystems. This chapter has sought to provide a potential systemic account of the parameters that control and determine the actual manifestations of person forms in discourse.

Observed from the traditional perspective, the grammatical category of person is typically related to independent personal pronouns; in this book, however, various realizations of the concept of person are taken into account, and their formal and functional properties are a major concern for this study.

The graphic notation of the system network developed by Halliday is a powerful tool that illustrates how semantic options are presented and made in the organization of language as meaning potential. With the aid of this set of symbols and rules, the complex system of person is presented in a disassembled manner as the account of intersecting subsystems unfolds. Figure 3.19 is an attempt to put what has been addressed together to represent the possible ways humans construe their experience in regard to their roles in verbal communication.

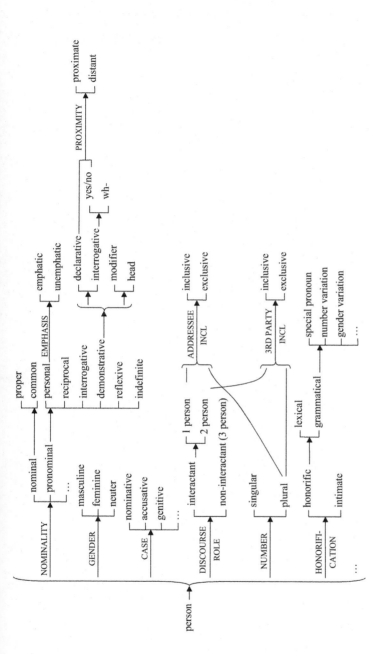

Figure 3.19 Synthesized system of person

Notes

1 This sample sentence is quoted from Laurence J. Peter.
2 *Neun* is used when the preceding syllable ends with a vocalic sound, while *eun* follows a consonant.
3 The change in topic also results in a change in definiteness (Martin, 1996: 231).

4 Lexicalization and grammaticalization of person

As has been discussed in the previous chapter, the system of person is concerned with identification of and reference to the participant roles in discourse. It is commonly encoded by nominal and pronominal expressions; however, cross-linguistically, other resources of language as meaning potential can perform the function as well, be they lexical or grammatical. In this chapter, a descriptive analysis of lexicalization and grammaticalization of the system of person is conducted with data drawn from a wide range of languages. From a typological point of view, the construal of a certain aspect of meaning (person in this case) achieves the same end by adopting diversified means in different languages, especially in genetically unrelated ones.

This chapter is composed of four sections. Section 4.1 addresses the lexical realization of person; Section 4.2 provides an account of the grammatical means for indicating person, among which personal pronouns stand out as an important and pervasive instrument, and at the same time a problematic one. Thus, personal pronouns are discussed at length in a separate section – Section 4.3. And Section 4.4 is a coda which summarizes this chapter.

4.1 Lexicalization of person

4.1.1 A note on lexis and lexicalization

4.1.1.1 Lexis

Lexis, also known as lexical items or lexical units, are words or chain of words as the basic elements in a language's lexicon, which, in linguistics, means the language's inventory of lexemes. "Lexical units" in morphology refers to the open-class morphemes that accept addition of new items, carry the primary information load of an utterance and are generally variable in form. Typically, lexical items include nouns, verbs, adjectives and adverbs. They are also called content words in traditional grammar, as opposed to function words, grammatical words or synsemantic words, which are of a closed-class type.

Lexis is also a key concern in many linguistic theories and applications, such as Chomskyan generative theory (Chomsky, 1981), lexical semantics (Lyons, 1977), lexicography (Sinclair, 1987), corpus linguistics (Hoey, 1993; Stubbs, 1996), first and second language acquisition (Clark, 1993), literary stylistics (Carter & Burton, 1982), the mental lexicon in cognitive linguistics (Lakoff, 1987), etc.

Examined from the perspective of Systemic Functional Linguistics (SFL), lexis is seen as one end of the lexicogrammar continuum. *An Introduction to Functional Grammar* (3rd ed.) gives a brief description of lexis: by "starting at the lexical end – with the 'content words' of the vocabulary – we find names of entities, names of processes and names of qualities" (Halliday & Matthiessen, 2004: 37). Entities, processes and qualities are hereupon adopted as features denoted by lexis as per SFL practice.

4.1.1.2 Lexicalization

The term "lexicalization" is used within linguistics to cover a rather extensive range of distinctive and yet related meanings (Bakken, 2006). They may be listed as follows:

(a) Lexicalization may refer to the expression of concepts by a lexical form. A certain concept may be lexicalized in one or some languages, but not necessarily so in others.
(b) Lexicalization may refer to the process of giving a lexical form to a new concept in a language and making it part of that language's lexicon. This is relevant to many word-formation processes, such as borrowing, blending, coinage, etc.
(c) Lexicalization can be viewed as the process in which morphological, syntactic or pragmatic means of language organization are taken over by lexis. This happens in certain forms of grammatical metaphor where a relation is construed through a process or an entity.
(d) Lexicalization may also be used in contrast to grammaticalization. The two processes are movements toward opposite directions along the lexis-grammar cline where meaning is construed. Hopper and Traugott (1993: 49) see it as a "process whereby a non-lexical form . . . becomes a fully referential lexical item."

In the account of lexicalization of person in this study, the term is basically used in accordance with (a) above, i.e. as the expression of the concept of person through a lexical form. When the issue of person-related meaning's movement along the lexis-grammar cline is addressed, the term "lexicalization" may be used in conformity with the meaning in (d), to indicate a movement in opposition to grammaticalization. It may also sometimes bear the meaning in (c) when cross-linguistic comparisons are drawn.

4.1.2 Lexicalization: entity

4.1.2.1 Nominal group indicating the third person

A participant role in discourse is most congruently identified and referred to by a nominal group since it is by nature an entity which can be either someone or

Lexicalization and grammaticalization 59

something. In most cases, nominal groups (including common and proper nouns) are employed to denote the third party that is neither the addresser nor the addressee. In languages where there is morphological inflection for the third person discourse role, the nominal groups show corresponding agreement in accordance with their syntactic status or require other constituents of the clause to keep in concord. Example 4.1 provides examples from Chinese, English and Latin respectively.

Example 4.1 Third person nominal group

(a) 山顶洞人　　　发现　　于　　北京　　周口店　　　山顶洞。
Upper cave men　discover　LOC　Beijing　Zhoukoudian　Upper cave
"Upper cave men were discovered at the Upper cave of Zhoukoudian, Beijing."

(b) **Amaranta** has **two brothers**.

(c) **Agricolae　　　cōnsilia　　　　　cōgitant.**
farmer PL NOM　plan PL ACC　　　ponder 3 PL PRES
"The farmers are pondering the plans."

Nominal groups identifying the third person are 山顶洞人 in (a), *Amaranta* and *two brothers* in (b) and *agricolae* and *cōnsilia* in (c). The third person singular proper noun *Amaranta* in (b) requires a special morphological ending on the process/verb *have* to achieve the agreement. In (c), the common nouns *agricola* and *cōnsilium* need to undergo proper morphological declensions according to the number, (grammatical) gender and syntactic roles (case), and, again, the process/verb should agree with the discourse role and number of the subject.

Despite the fact that 北京周口店山顶洞 in (a) is also a nominal group, the preposition 于 makes it a Circumstance: Location instead of a participant in this clause. Therefore, it is not treated as taking any participant role, hence is irrelevant to the topic of third person under discussion.

As is seen above, the third person discourse role of nominal groups is quite patent and self-evident, and thus it should receive no further account in this section. The third person can be recognized as the unmarked realization of nominal groups. In contrast to this, the first and second person participant roles are normally performed by grammatical means such as personal pronouns; however, there are certain occasions where nominal groups are used to play the first and second person roles as well.

4.1.2.2 Nominal group indicating the first person

In some circumstances the first person reference can be realized by nominal groups. Consider the following examples in Chinese classics:

Example 4.2 Nominal group denoting the first person

(a) 予　　　小子　　　　既　　　获　　　仁人，
　　I　　little child　　PERF　obtain　virtuous men

60 *Lexicalization and grammaticalization*

敢　　　祇承　　　　　上帝，
dare　comply with　God
以　　　遏　　　　　乱略。（《尚书·周书·武成》）
so as to　stop　　　disorder

"I, the little child, having obtained (the help of) virtuous men, presume reverently to comply with (the will of) God, and make an end of his disorderly ways." (Successful completion of the war, "Zhou Shu," *Shang Shu*)[1]

(b) 诸人　　持议，　　甚　　　失　　孤　　　　望。
　　people　proposal　much　dis...　lonely man　...appoint
（《资治通鉴》卷六十五）

"People's proposals greatly disappointed me." (Vol. 65, *Comprehensive Mirror for Aid in Government*)

(c) 今　　　天下　　　　　　　　英雄，
　　now　under heaven　　　　　hero
　　惟　　　使君　　　　　　　　　　与　　操　　耳。
　　none...　provincial civil official　and　Cao　...but
（《三国演义》第二十一回）

"The only heroes in the world are you and I." (Chapter 21, *Romance of the Three Kingdoms*)[2]

In the above quotations none of the boldfaced first person terms is pronominal; instead, they are either common nouns (as in (a) and (b)) or proper noun (as in (c)). This is indeed not an unusual phenomenon in traditional Chinese literature and people's way of referring to themselves.

Most of the first person nominal terms in Chinese are used to express self-degradation or humbleness. In Example 4.2(a) the term 小子 literally means "a little child" but is used by Ji Fa, the first king of the Zhou Dynasty (1046–256 B.C.), as a self-reference. 孤 in Example 4.2(b) refers to "an orphan" or "a lonely man" literally; however, it is typically employed as a first person-indicating humble term by feudal kings.

Interestingly, such originally humble terms began to carry a meaning that shows a power relation when they were designated as self-address expressions used exclusively by the condescending people in power, such as emperors, kings and high-ranking officials. Such pseudo-humble terms also include 寡人, 朕 (before it was grammaticalized as a first person pronoun which is also exclusive to emperors), 孤家, 孤王, etc.

Genuine self-referring humble terms usually incorporate appraisal (especially attitude: judgment: negative) elements to show one's incompetence, humbleness, inferiority, ignorance, immaturity, senility, etc., such as 小可, 小人 (little man); 鄙人, 敝人 (vulgar/humble man); 仆 (slave); 愚兄, 愚弟 (foolish brother); 晚辈 (junior); 老夫 (old man); and so on. On other occasions the speakers refer to themselves using their occupation or social position, optionally combined with attitude-invoking elements, such as 臣 (minister); 妾 (concubine); 奴才 (slave); 下官, 末官, 小吏 (inferior official); 小生, 晚生 (young scholar); 贫僧 (poor Buddhist monk); 贫道 (poor Taoist monk);[3] etc. These self-references form an

Lexicalization and grammaticalization 61

open-class set, and there is no fixed limit to the repertoire. This type of self-reference is found in English, too.

Example 4.3 *The Humble Petition of Bruar Water*, by Robert Burns (excerpted)

> My lord, I know, your noble ear
> Woe ne'er assails in vain;
> Embolden'd thus, I beg you'll hear
> **Your humble slave** complain,
> How saucy Phoebus' scorching beams,
> In flaming summer-pride,
> Dry-withering, waste my foamy streams,
> And drink my crystal tide.

Through the use of common nouns denoting social roles or identities to refer to oneself, a sense of intimacy can be produced when the addresser bears a higher position than the addressee. This is typically found in baby-talk, as in Example 4.4.

Example 4.4 First person nominal reference showing intimacy

(a) 孩子， 听话， **奶奶** 给 你 讲 故事。
    kid   be obedient granny BEN you tell story
    "Kid, be good, Granny's telling you a story."
(b) Tommy, be quiet, **daddy**'s gonna tell you a story.

Or distance is created between the addresser and addressee, as in Example 4.5. Note that this is not the humble type of self-reference with occupation or social status but a power-manifesting one.

Example 4.5 First person nominal reference creating distance/power relation

大家   坐好，   下面   **老师**   开始   发   试卷。
everyone sit properly next teacher   start hand out test paper.
"Sit up properly, everyone. I am (the teacher is) going to hand out test papers."

Another connotation that nominal groups functioning as a first person indicator can bring about is detachment of the addresser from the discourse. This nuance is especially required when the discourse is supposed to convey information with objectivity, authenticity and impartiality. And this is why it is found that so many academic theses are written with *the author*, *the writer* in English and with 作者, 笔者 in Chinese denoting the first person, instead of the subjective-sounding first person pronoun *I*.

Now recall the sample clause given in Example 4.2(c), where the addresser refers to himself with his given name. This is a conventional way of self-address in traditional Chinese speech. Traditional naming for men in China involves a

62 *Lexicalization and grammaticalization*

complex series of components: there is a surname (姓), a given name (名), a courtesy name (字) and sometimes a literary name (号) as well. For example, the founding father of the Chinese National People's Party (or Kuomintang) has the surname *Sun*, the given name *Wen*, the courtesy name *Yat-sen* and a literary name *Zhongshan*, with a child name *Dixiang*, another courtesy name *Zaizhi* and another literary name *Rixin*. Usually the given name is used for reference to oneself, in order to show an attitude of humbleness and modesty.

It is also noted that many celebrities in the circles of politics, sports or entertainment address themselves using their names (or nicknames) instead of the first person pronoun. It is increasingly commonplace to hear those stars refer to themselves in this way, as in Example 4.6.

Example 4.6 Celebrities' self-reference with proper name

(a) 范纬琪：能唱歌给你们听，是**范范**最开心的一件事情。(from her blog)
     "Wei Chi Fan:[4] It is the happiest thing for Fan Fan to be able to sing for you."
(b) Julia Gillard: . . . a reelected **Gillard** government will cut company tax . . . (address to the National Press Club Canberra)

In these cases the personalities seem to be detaching from themselves as a participant in the discourse, but they adopt the proper noun to represent themselves as the iconized image in public view.

The nominal groups used to indicate the first person discourse role are all in third person concord. This, as against the usual practice in which nominal groups express the third person role, could be viewed as a marked usage of person forms. Whenever a nominal group is used to denote the first person, there is some sort of socially or stylistically varied meaning according to the tenor of the context, in contrast to the unmarked usage of first person pronouns which more congruently express the addresser's discourse role.

4.1.2.3 *Nominal group indicating the second person*

The most commonly seen nominal groups indicating the second person would be vocatives, which are used in addressing or invoking participants in discourse. These vocatives comprise a considerable variety of types, some of which are listed and exemplified below.

(1) Personal name. Personal names are a nominal repertoire for addressing the second person across languages. Different types of names can be given to a person according to the naming system of a language. In English, for example, a person can be addressed by a first name, by a last name, by a pet name or by a nickname, or also by some combination of these. In traditional Chinese addressing practice, it is considered polite to address someone by the courtesy name.
(2) Title. Although the term "title" can sometimes be used for all nominal variants of address terms except personal names, here "title" refers to the form of

address which corresponds to the English *Mr./Mrs./Miss*, the Chinese 先生/太太/女士/小姐, the French *Monsieur/Madame/Mademoiselle*, etc. They again could be combined with personal names.
(3) Appointment and occupational terms. On many occasions appointment titles (e.g. *president, doctor*) and occupational terms indicating the addressee's profession (e.g. *driver, waiter*) can serve as vocative forms of address. However, there may be some language-specific tendencies in using these terms. For example, one would be more likely to address a vehicle operator with 司机 in Chinese than with *driver* in English.
(4) Kinship terms. These are also a kind of frequently used address term for familial members. However, kinship terms may sometimes be extended to people with no real blood relation, such as the use of 叔叔 (uncle) for any male person around one's father's age.
(5) Terms of endearment. In addressing beloved ones or small children, terms of endearment are often used, e.g. *sweetheart, sweet pea, darling, sugar, honey, baby*, etc. The list is almost endless because such terms are also an open class, and new members could be invented at any time with creativity and imagination. It is noteworthy that in certain contexts literally derogatory terms can also be used to show affection, e.g. *you little bastard* said by an old man to his beloved grandson.
(6) Other types of relationship. These include terms for other socially formed relationships such as *friend, neighbor, comrade* and so on. It is interesting to note how the neutral address term 同志 (comrade) is used in China. This term embodies no clear hint of power or solidarity and can be used alone or in various combinations, e.g. 同志 (no combination), 张俊杰同志 (Comrade Zhang Junjie, combined with personal name), 老同志 (old comrade, combined with Epithet), 老张同志 (old Comrade Zhang, combined with Epithet and personal name), 院长同志 (Comrade Dean, combined with appointment), etc. (see Scotton & Zhu, 1983).
(7) Abstract nominal groups. According to Braun (1988: 10), such terms of address are originally based on some abstract quality of the addressee, such as *Your Excellency, Your Grace, Your Honor*, etc. In Chinese, many such abstract nominal address terms derive from locations, e.g. 陛下 (Your Majesty, literally "underneath the throne"), 殿下 (Your Highness, literally "underneath the temple"), 阁下 (Your Excellency, literally "underneath the pavilion"), etc.

The above classifications of vocative second person nominal groups are far from exhaustive since nominals are by nature an open class and thus subject to addition or elimination as the language develops. Consider the example *Hey man!* Which type does the *man* fit into?

The non-vocative nominal groups indicating the second person, similar to nouns for the first person, may imply some special social meaning, especially power relations or social distance between the addresser and the addressee, or deference.

(a) Vocative *lady*

Mood structure				Vocative
Mood		Residue		
Finite	Subject	Predicator	Complement	
Do	you	have	any other order	**lady**

(b) Non-vocative *lady*

Mood structure			
Mood		Residue	
Finite	Subject	Predicator	Complement
Does	**the lady**	have	any other order

Figure 4.1 Vocative vs. non-vocative nominal participant

Some of the forms may coincide with the vocatives, but they ought to be differentiated because, along with vocatives, there tend to be other forms of second person expression in the clause, and a vocative address form is but an extension of the participant in the discourse instead of being "part of the proposition or proposal being negotiated" (Martin et al., 1997, cited from Gouveia, 2007) and thus "outside the scope of Mood and Residue" (Halliday & Matthiessen, 2004: 133) (though Gouveia (2007) argues otherwise),[5] while non-vocative nominal groups are immediate participants in the clause/negotiation. A comparison is drawn between vocative and non-vocative in terms of Mood structure in Figure 4.1.

And Example 4.7 offers more examples of non-vocative nominal groups indicating the second person.

Example 4.7 Non-vocative second person nominal group

(a) 我　　住　　长江　　　　头，
    I　　live　Yangtze River　head
    君　　住　　长江　　　　尾。（李之仪《卜算子》）
    gentleman　live　Yangtze River　tail
    "I live at the head of Yangtze River; you live at the tail of it." (*To the Tune of Busuanzi*, by Li Zhiyi)

(b) （曹操）　欠身　　谓　　云长　　　曰：
    Cao　　　bow　　say　　Yunchang　PROJ
    "将军　　别来　　　　无恙？"（《三国演义》第五十回）
    general　since parted　be well
    "(Cao Cao) rode out to the front, bowed low and said, 'General, I trust you have enjoyed good health.'" (Chapter 50, *Romance of the Three Kingdoms*)[2]

(c) I yet beseech **Your Majesty**, if for I want that glib and oily art.
    　　　　　　　　　　(*King Lear*, Act One, Scene One, Lines 230-231)

In Japanese, it is a very common phenomenon to use nominal groups in place of second person pronouns although there is a whole set of such pronouns, like *anata, kimi, kisama* and *omae*. The Japanese simply avoid using them. Wang (2003) holds that it is largely due to the historical reasons underlying the formation of second person pronouns and the hierarchical characteristics of the Japanese society. Second person pronouns in Japanese have rather a short history, and some of them were not grammaticalized as pronouns until the 16th century. On the other hand, second person pronouns are not used because they are not considered capable enough of expressing various social and interpersonal relationships. The "deep-rooted traditional culture endows the Japanese with a fixed way of thinking; i.e. if you neglect social differences, using 'you' to refer to everyone, then, your behavior is not in accordance with your position, the Japanese will say" (Wang, 2003: 94). Example 4.8(a) is taken from a dialogue between two elementary school pupils; (b) is a comment made to the elder one of two teenage sisters by a middle-aged woman. It is difficult to translate them into English or Chinese without explicit usage of the second personal pronoun *you*.

> Example 4.8 Nominal group in place of second person pronoun in Japanese (Wang, 2003)
>
> (a) **Tama san** wa   okasan ni   nani   ageru no?
>   Tama HON TOP   mother BEN   what   give INT
>   "What will you (Tama) give to your mother?"
> (b) **Onesan** wa   furansu ningyou   mitai ne.
>   elder sister TOP   French doll   look like EXM
>   "You (the elder sister) look so much like a French doll!"

In contrast to nominal groups, the use of second person pronouns in Japanese is virtually restricted to dialogues between husband and wife or between very close friends, or a superior addressing a subordinate. "The main rule of thumb about pronouns in Japanese is to avoid them completely in every polite conversation, and to avoid them as much as possible everywhere else" (McClure, 2000: 234).

Similar to Japanese, the Korean language also prefers nominal groups to second person pronouns in addressing people with higher social status, although a good number of the latter can be found in Korean, such as *dangsin, jane, neo* and so on. See Example 4.9.

> Example 4.9 Nominal group in place of second person pronoun in Korean (Lee & Ramsey, 2000: 244)
>
> **Halabeoji** neun   don i   iss euseyo?
> grandfather TOP   money NOM   have HON
> "Do you (grandfather) have money?"

According to Lee and Ramsey (2000: 94), second person pronouns are "normally not used to refer to someone who must be respected; there are many instances

66 *Lexicalization and grammaticalization*

where one can only use a noun to refer to such a person." Therefore, in the above example, there is no way for *grandfather* to be replaced with a pronoun. Another explanation for this characteristic of Korean (and also of Japanese) is that "it is a language in which pronominalization is not as active a process as it is in other languages" (ibid.).

4.1.3 Lexicalization: process

It is common in many languages for the meaning of a participant role to be integrated into a process by means of the verb conjugation. However, such a denotation of person would be a grammatical means instead of a lexical one. The lexicalization of person through uninflected verbs is indeed rare. But in Japanese there are quite a good number of such verbs incorporating the concept of person.

In Japanese, some verbs of giving and receiving have "an intrinsic directionality which helps to identify the person performing the act of giving" (Lange, 1988: 502). Giving and receiving, as two aspects of exchanging goods and services, have the same three participants in the clause: a "giver," a "receiver" and "goods-&-services." The "goods-&-services" being exchanged are construed as Goal in both types, while the "giver" and "receiver" are construed differently. In a giving process, the giver is the Actor and the receiver is the Recipient, but in a receiving process, the receiver is construed as the Actor and the giver as the Recipient. Both types are modeled by material clauses of extension (Teruya, 2006: 302–303).

The five most frequently occurring verbs for giving in Japanese are *kudasaru*, *kureru*, *sashiageru*, *ageru* and *yaru*.

Kudasaru and *kureru* mean "giving by someone other than the speaker to the speaker or a member of the speaker's in-group"; *kudasaru* implies that the giver has a higher social position than the speaker or that the speaker feels it necessary to show respect for the giver, while *kureru* is an unmarked form implying that the giver is equal or inferior to the receiver.

Example 4.10 Japanese giving verb implying person

(a) Koucha wo   **kudasa**-i.
    black tea ACC   give-IMP
    "Please give me some black tea."
(b) Tomodachi ga   purezento wo   **kure**-mashi-ta.
    friend NOM   present ACC   give-HON-PAST
    "My friend gave me a present."

In both clauses in Example 4.10, there is no explicit form for a participant that receives the goods, but the first person Recipient is indicated by the choice of verb alone.

In contrast, *sashiageru*, *ageru* and *yaru* mean "giving something to someone other than the speaker"; *sashiageru* is used when the giver is inferior to the receiver, *ageru* is used in describing giving to an equal or a superior with an

Lexicalization and grammaticalization 67

intrinsic element of politeness to the receiver, and *yaru* is the unmarked form that lacks the politeness used in an informal and plain manner.

Example 4.11 Japanese giving verb implying person

(a) Okasan ni **age**-te.
mother BEN give-IMP
"Give it to your mother."

(b) Kare wa inu ni esa wo **ya**-tta.
he TOP dog BEN food ACC give-PAST
"He fed the dog."

Again, the giving verbs require that the beneficiary/receiver not be a first person; therefore, it would be plainly wrong to produce an utterance like that in Example 4.12.

Example 4.12 Mismatched giving verb and beneficiary

*Kanojo wa watashi ni kudamono wo **age**-ta.
she TOP me BEN fruit ACC give-PAST
"She gave me some fruit."

Likewise, the humble receiving verb *itadaku* means "something is received by the first person speaker or by a member of the speaker's in-group," and thus it is not used on occasions where "you/he/she/it/they receive(s)" something unless the second or third person receiver is an inferior member of the speaker's in-group, especially when the giver is present.

Some verbs in Japanese have special honorific and humble equivalents, used in accordance with the addresser's attitude to the addressee or topic of the clause. Honorific verbs are used by raising the status of the subject, and thus they indicate a participant role of the second or third person, never the first. Humble verbs are used to lower the addresser's status, so they are always associated with the addresser or a member of his/her in-group, most of the time denoting the first person role in the discourse. For instance, *Go annai itashimasu* is always interpreted as *I will show you the way*, although the first person *I* is not explicit in the discourse but is embodied by the choice of the verb *itasu*. The lexicalization of person within the Process is a prominent feature of the "honorific language" in Japanese. See Table 4.1 for a few more examples.

Table 4.1 Honorific and humble verbs in Japanese

Neutral	Honorific (-1st person)	Humble (+1st person)
suru "do"	*nasaru*	*itasu*
iu "say"	*ossharu*	*mousu, moushiageru*
taberu "eat"	*meshiagaru*	*itadaku*
iku "go"	*irassharu*	*mairu*

4.1.4 Lexicalization: quality

4.1.4.1 Adjective

Typically, adjectives function as the Post-deictic, Numerative, Classifier or Epithet in a nominal group, specifying the attribute of a noun. However, on some occasions, the noun modified by the adjective can be omitted, which makes the adjective look like a noun (Thing in SFL terminology), and it can then be preceded by a determiner though it does not otherwise meet the criteria that typically distinguish a lexical item as a noun, such as plurality in English, e.g. *the poor* vs. **the poors*.

The resemblance of such adjectives to nouns enables them to identify or refer to participant roles in discourse as nouns commonly do, and the unmarked reference would be the third person as can be predicted. In English, the definite determiner *the* is usually combined with such adjectives, and these adjectives are in a plural concordance with the verb if they are the Subject.

> Example 4.13 Adjective indicating third person participant role
>
> (a) The **sick** and the **wounded** were sent home.
> (b) The **rich** are privileged.
> (c) They offered help to the **homeless**.
> (d) 使　　老　　有所　　终，
>   make　old　have means　end
>   壮　　　　有所　　用，
>   grown-up　have means　employ
>   幼　　　　有所　　长。（《礼记·礼运》）
>   young　　have means　grow
>   "A competent provision was secured for the aged till their death, employment for the able-bodied, and the means of growing up to the young" ("Li Yun," *The Book of Rites*)⁶
> (e) **旧的**　不　　去，　**新的**　不　　来。
>   old　NEG　go　　new　　NEG　come
>   "The new won't come until the old go."

Adjectives indicating the first and the second person can be found, too, although they are far fewer than nouns with the same function. In Chinese, some adjectives with negative attitude are often employed to refer to oneself in literary works or formal writing, such as 不才 (good for nothing), 不肖 (unworthy), 小的 (little), 老朽 (old and worthless), 老拙 (old and clumsy) and so on. These humble and self-degrading adjectival terms are also nominalized and function as participants in discourse.

Adjectives referring to the second person are generally used as vocatives, most of which are presumably terms of endearment involving positive judgment, such as 亲爱的 in Chinese, *dear* in English, *chère* in French, etc. Occasionally adjectives other than endearment terms are used as vocatives, as in Example 4.14.

Example 4.14 Adjective indicating the second person

但是，	**聪明的,**	你	告诉	我,
but	clever	you	tell	me

我们的	日子	为什么	一	去	不	复返	呢 ?(朱自清《匆匆》)
we GEN	day	why	once	go	NEG	return	INT

"Now, you the wise, tell me, why should our days leave us, never to return?" (*Rush*, by Zhu Ziqing)[7]

4.1.4.2 *Adverb*

Adverbs, or adverbial groups, typically modify the meaning of an adjective, a verb, another adverb or even a whole clause and typically express time, place, degree, manner, etc. Within the systemic functional framework, adverbial groups usually function as Adjuncts or Circumstantial elements.

It may seem extremely unlikely that such a lexical item as an adverb can actually indicate any person role in a discourse; however, the Spanish words *conmigo* (with me), *contigo* (with you) and *consigo* (with oneself) look in every way like adverbs although they derive from the combination of the preposition *con* and the objective forms of personal pronouns. Consider Example 4.15.

Example 4.15 Adverb indicating person role

¿Puedo	ir	**contigo**?
can-1 SG PRES	go	with you

"Can I go with you?"

The lexical item *contigo* modifies the verb *ir* and expresses how the process is carried out. If not contracted, the preposition *con*, corresponding to English *with*, is said to be "extensively used to form adverbial phrases of manner" (Kattán-Ibarra & Pountain, 2003: 119); however, the contracted forms are generally treated as personal pronouns, either as "objective pronouns"[8] (Bosque & Demonte, 1999: 1219) or what is simply called "special forms" of pronouns (Kattán-Ibarra & Pountain, 2003: 37).

According to Halliday and Matthiessen (2004: 272–273), joint participation in the process represented by Circumstance: Accompaniment, which is a Circumstantial element typically realized by prepositional phrases with prepositions such as *with, without, besides*. The lexicalized Circumstance: Accompaniment in Spanish can by no means be seen as a "prepositional phrase"; instead, the most appropriate class label should be none other than "adverbial," which typically functions as a circumstantial element of Location, Manner, etc. There is indeed no reason to regard them as "pronouns." Thus, the lexical items *conmigo, contigo* and *consigo* are best classified as "adverbs of accompaniment" when their function is duly taken into account. As a matter of fact, some – though still few – Spanish teaching materials and dictionaries have labeled their word class as adverb.[9]

As is stated in Section 4.1.2.1, circumstantial elements are usually not viewed as being relevant to participant roles in discourse, but the lexicalized circumstance to which person roles are fused deserves special treatment. The process actually has two participants with both entities sharing the same participant function, except that one of them is represented circumstantially (Halliday & Matthiessen, 2004: 273), which gives the other textual prominence and interpersonal negotiability.

4.2 Grammaticalization of person

4.2.1 A note on grammar and grammaticalization

4.2.1.1 Grammar

Grammar in linguistics means the set of structural rules that govern the composition of linguistic structures in language, such as clauses, phrases, words, etc. It can also refer to the study and description of such rules, as in "Generative Grammar" or "Functional Grammar." In SFL, grammar is also treated as one end of the cline of lexicogrammar, the stratum of language organization realizing semantics and realized by phonology/graphology.

In the binary classification of word classes, grammatical categories are separated from lexical categories. Grammatical words are those that serve to express grammatical relationships between linguistic elements or specify meanings other than concrete entities, processes and qualities. This notional distinction is rooted in the works of Greek and Roman grammarians. Sapir (1921: 82–89) has made a broad distinction between "concrete concepts" (including objects, actions and qualities) and "relational concepts" (including reference, modality, personal relations, number, time, etc.), which largely corresponds to the opposition between lexical and grammatical words.

Grammatical words include pronouns, prepositions, conjunctions, auxiliaries, determiners, particles, etc., all of which belong to closed-class groups because it is very uncommon to have new such function words created in language. And they tend not to be isolated from content words in discourse.

Interestingly, grammatical words may also have characteristic phonological properties as against lexical ones. For example, only grammatical words can begin with the voiced dental fricative /ð/ in English.

4.2.1.2 Grammaticalization

In linguistics, grammaticalization (or sometimes grammaticization) is generally regarded as "a process by which linguistic elements (lexical, pragmatic, and sometimes even phonetic items) change into constituents of grammar, or by which grammatical items become more grammatical in time" (Wischer, 2006), or "the process whereby lexical items and constructions come in certain linguistic contexts to serve grammatical functions, and, once grammaticalized, continue to develop new grammatical functions" (Hopper & Traugott, 2003: xv). The most common example in the grammaticalization literature would be the development of the auxiliary *going to* in English from the lexical verb *go*. Simply put, grammaticalization means the process by which a lexical item loses some or all of its lexical meaning and begins to perform a grammatical function.

It is noted that the above definitions of grammaticalization seem to focus too intensely on its diachronic aspect. It is viewed as a mobile process across time, developing from the lexis end to the grammatical end. Nonetheless, grammaticalization can also be observed from a synchronic perspective. It can be seen as "primarily a morpho-syntactic, discourse pragmatic phenomenon, to be studied from the point of view of fluid, dynamic patterns of language use at a moment in time" (Brinton & Traugott, 2005: 22), or "a synchronic state of coding of grammatical categories, such as case, number, gender, tense, aspect, mood, etc." (Wischer, 2006:129). Again, to put it more simply, grammaticalization can refer to the expression of a concept by a grammatical form, corresponding to item (a) in the list of meanings of lexicalization in 4.1.1.2.

There are various forms of grammaticalized concepts. Some of them are independent words, and some are not independent but must be bound or attached to other elements as clitics, affixes or other categories. Some of the grammatical concepts may not even have an explicit form in discourse. And it should also be noted again that the same conceptual phenomenon may be construed cross-linguistically by either lexical means or grammatical means, or different degrees of either, or both.

As far as grammaticalization is concerned, it is helpful to use a model of a continuum with various clusters or focal areas of different grammatical forms (see Halliday, 1961: 249). Hopper and Traugott (1993: 5–7) developed a "cline of grammaticality" of the following type:

content item > grammatical word > clitic > inflectional affix

with grammatical forms including (1) grammatical words with relative phonological and syntactic independence, (2) derivational forms, (3) clitics and (4) inflections.

Various other schemata of grammaticalization are also presented, such as:

discourse > syntax > morphology > morphophonemics > zero (Givón, 1979: 209)
lexicon > elexicalization > morphologization > morphology (Ramat, 2001: 394)
phrase > compound > derivation > inflection (Brinton & Traugott, 2005: 86)

4.2.2 Grammaticalization of person: an overview

Grammaticalized person markers may adopt various morpho-phonological forms, which perform different syntactic functions and have different distribution patterns cross-linguistically. The grammatical person forms that are closest to lexical items are independent forms, typically personal pronouns, which constitute individual words and may take primary stress. As personal pronouns manifest quite complex features rather than being clear-cut and straightforward, they will be accounted for in a separate section (4.3).

In contrast, dependent person forms cannot receive primary word stress; typically they are morphologically and orthographically dependent on other elements, phonologically reduced and/or restricted in distribution. Siewierska (2004) distinguishes four types of dependent person markers:

> Dependent person markers may be classified on the basis of their decreasing morphological independence and phonological substance into ... four types: weak > clitic > bound > zero.
>
> (21–22)

Weak forms of person markers, according to Siewierska (2004: 34), are like independent forms, but they are "not just unstressed versions of independent forms but rather differ from them both phonologically and in terms of syntactic distribution." She also comments that "the notion of weak form or weak pronoun is not firmly established in the literature and therefore there is no consensus on the type of properties that weak forms should display" (ibid.: 36–37). French is a language that is said to have weak forms of person markers, i.e. the *je* group (for subjects) and *me* group (for objects) as opposed to the *moi* group used as independent and stressed strong pronouns, but they are generally analyzed as clitics. Due to the controversial status of the so-called weak person forms, it is advisable to exclude them from the account in the present study.

"Bound form of person markers" is also a problematic term in that it is "often used in the literature as a cover term for both person affixes and clitics" (Siewierska, 2004: 24). In Siewierska (2004) the term "bound form" is used chiefly for person markers expressed by affixes or by changes to the stem. In the present study, such person forms are simply called affixes.

Therefore, in this study, the grammatical means for realizing the concept of person follow the cline represented below, with clitics, affixes and zero forms to be accounted for in this section.

personal pronoun > clitic > affix > zero form

4.2.3 Grammaticalization: clitic

Clitics are morphemes that share properties of both inflectional affixes and independent words and that at the same time are different from both and need to be distinguished from either. They "present analytic difficulties because they are neither clearly independent words nor clearly affixes" (Zwicky, 1977: 1). Phonologically, clitics resemble inflectional affixes in that they generally do not take the stress and have to form a tonic group with their host; orthographically, clitics may look like independent words because they are written separately in some languages and/or on some occasions, or they look like affixes when they are attached to the host in writing. Many efforts have been made in defining clitics and distinguishing them from inflectional affixes on the one hand and from independent words on the other (see Zwicky, 1977, 1985, 1987, 1994; Zwicky & Pullum, 1983).

The essence of understanding clitics is that they function at the word group rank instead of word rank, and a clitic always has a host to attach to. A clitic preceding a host is called a proclitic, and one following a host an enclitic. Zwicky (1985) makes a distinction between "simple clitics" and "special clitics"; the former "serve as reduced forms occurring in the same positions as corresponding full forms" such as the English auxiliaries *'d, 's*, etc., while the latter are those "not partaking of the distribution of corresponding full forms," such as the Latin conjunctive – *que*, etc. It has become a convention to make this distinction following Zwicky's works.

When it comes to the clitics indicating person roles in discourse, simple clitics are reduced forms of personal pronouns that occur in the same position and perform exactly the same function as the associated full forms, such as in colloquial and connected speech in English, as shown by the bold type letters in Example 4.16.

Example 4.16 Simple clitics

(a) Tell**'er** the truth.
    "Tell her the truth."
(b) Give**'em** back to me.
    "Give them back to me."

Special clitics, on the other hand, either have no corresponding full forms or do not have the same distribution patterns as their corresponding full forms do. They are rather independent compared with full forms in terms of phonological, morphological and syntactic properties. Major attention should be focused on special clitics in the study of clitics. Here are a few examples from Spanish.

Example 4.17 Special clitics

(a) **Me**   lave   la cara.
    1 SG REFL CLT   wash-1 SG PAST the face
    "I washed my face."
(b) **Te**   **me**   recomendó.
    2 SG DAT CLT   1 SG ACC CLT   recommend-3 SG PAST
    "He/she recommended me to you."
(c) Dá**melo**!
    give-IMP^1 SG DAT CLT^3 SG ACC CLT
    "Give it to me!"

The clitic *me* in Example 4.17(a) looks like a separate word, but actually it is dependent on its host verb *lavar* and functions at the rank of the verbal group. It can never occur alone, nor can it take primary stress. At the same time, it also has some relative independence in that it is written separately from its host. However, in its original non-finite form *lavarse*, the enclitic *se* does not attain such relative

74 *Lexicalization and grammaticalization*

independence but is glued to its host verb, which may make it look similar to a suffix. But still the clitic *se* functions as a Participant and is more independent than an affix. The relatively unrestricted nature in terms of position and morphological status is what makes special clitics special.

In Example 4.17(b) and (c), there are each two personal clitics, which are grouped together with the host finite verb and identify the participant roles in the clause. They are still neither independent personal pronouns nor affixes, but the sequence between the two clitics is restricted owing to their respective syntactic functions.

In traditional grammar, such clitics in Romance languages are sometimes termed "unstressed pronouns," "dependent pronouns," "reflexive pronouns," etc. As a matter of fact, not only are the marked forms of dependent pronouns such as objective or reflexive ones in Romance languages seen as clitics, e.g. *me*, *te*, *se* in French, but the unmarked forms for subjects can be regarded as clitics too, since they meet each and every criterion there is for clitics. For example, in the French clause *Je t'aime* (I love you), the subject *je* can also be classified as a clitic just like the uncontroversial *t'*, because it is also unstressed and dependent on the verb, never able to stand alone.

In summary, cliticization of person forms is a further grammaticalization process compared with independent personal pronouns. While clitics still retain some kind of flexibility as well as losing some, affixation, a still further step toward grammaticalization, loses more independence and the participant role indicator becomes phonologically and graphologically fixed in relation to the process of the clause.

4.2.4   *Grammaticalization: affix*

Identification of participant roles, i.e. person, can be reflected by inflectional affixes, the most common forms of which are verbal conjugation suffixes, typically found in the Indo-European languages. Through the process of conjugation, a verb can derive from its dictionary entry form (or "principal part" following Latinate tradition) a set of inflected forms that may indicate number, gender, tense, aspect, mood, voice and the grammatical person, etc.

A conjugation paradigm is helpful in learning languages with such a grammatical information creation process. For example, in Latin, a verb in the present tense, active voice and indicative mood is conjugated with the suffixes *-ō*, *-s*, *-t*, *-mus*, *-tis* and *-nt* according to the participant role and number. Thus, from the ending *-mus* in the finite verb form *vocamus* (we call), the participant of the process is known to be *we*. See Table 4.2 for a conjugation paradigm.

Table 4.2 Person-indicating suffixes for the Latin verb *vocō*

	Singular	Plural
1	vocō	vocā**mus**
2	vocās	vocā**tis**
3	vocat	voca**nt**

Unlike many other Indo-European languages, which can inflect verbs for various grammatical systems with complex conjugation paradigms, English has reduced verb conjugation to a large extent. Most finite uses of verbs in Modern English do not show any information about the participant, except that the third person singular in the present tense is indicated by a relic *-s*. A fuller conjugation paradigm is used for the verb *be*, which makes a distinction among the three persons in the singular in the present tense, i.e. *am, are, is*.

The integration of participant roles within the Process by inflectional suffixes may not necessitate the explicit coding of the participant. In English the declarative mood is realized by Subject^Finite, both of which are obligatory; however, in languages like Spanish and Italian where inflectional suffixes reveal person roles, the Subject, be it nominal or pronominal, can be optional and made implicit in discourse, as in Example 4.18.

Example 4.18 Person reflected by inflectional suffix in Spanish and Italian

(a) **Tienes** razón.
 have-2 SG PRES reason
 "You have reason." / "You are right."
(b) **Hai** ragione.
 have-2 SG PRES reason
 "You have reason." / "You are right."

In French, however, the Subject is always required although the verb is always conjugated and is denoting the participant. Thus, *tu as raison* in French would mean the same as the above clauses in Spanish and Italian, with *as* (you have) inflected indicating the second person and *tu* (you) still explicitly there as Subject. This kind of redundancy of subjective personal pronouns in French – *je, tu, il/elle, nous, vous, ils/elles* – makes them look like clitics rather than fully independent pronouns, as is discussed in the previous subsection.

Naturally, the optionality of subjective personal pronouns in languages like Spanish and Italian means that such pronouns can also be present in a clause, such as the Spanish *tú tienes razón*, but it is an extremely marked usage of the personal pronoun, to give the addressee *tú* a prominent thematic position and emphasis. It does not alter the ideational meaning at all, nor does it seriously affect the interpersonal meaning, but it renders a different kind of textual implication.

Apart from suffixes, other types of inflectional affixes indicating person, i.e. prefixes, infixes and circumfixes, are very rare and not found in major languages in the world. A brief report is given in Siewierska (2004: 24–26).

It should be noted that inflectional affixes have been incorporated into the verb and thus become one part of it. They function at the rank of word and represent a more general grammatical feature. They are fixed, inflexible and fully dependent on the verb, and hence they are envisaged as taking a further step toward the grammaticalization end.

4.2.5 Grammaticalization: zero form

If the cline of grammaticalization of person is further extended, zero person forms might be viewed as the ultimate state of grammaticalization, developing all the way from fully independent personal pronouns, clitics and affixes. Siewierska (2004: 22) defines a zero person form as "a grammatical person interpretation without any accompanying phonological form of any type be it segmental or suprasegmental." The absence of phonological form can be understood as an implicit marker of person on some restricted occasions in English, such as the unmarked realization of the imperative mood, e.g. Example 4.19(a); ellipsis across clauses, e.g. Example 4.19(b); non-finite clauses, e.g. Example 4.19(c); and at times declarative clauses in informal and colloquial usage, e.g. Example 4.19(d).

Example 4.19 Zero person forms in English

(a) Φ Get out!
(b) John hugged Mary and Φ left.
(c) Sara stood in the lobby, Φ talking to her husband.
(d) Φ Wasn't home yesterday.

The participants in the empty positions can be interpreted as referring to *you*, *John*, *Sara* and *I* respectively.

Chinese allows a more flexible use of zero person forms, with the subjects elided when they are retrievable from the context of the situation. Consider the dialogue in Example 4.20, showing two persons talking via an online instant messaging tool.

Example 4.20 Zero person forms in Chinese

A: Φ 在   吗？
       be   INT
    "Are you there?"
B: Φ 在。
       be
    "I'm here."
A: Φ 在   做   什么   呢？
       PROG do   what   INT
    "What are you doing?"
B: Φ 看   电影   呢。
       watch movie   PROG
    "I'm watching a movie."

The participants can be made explicit if speaker A uses 你 (you) and speaker B 我 (I). The elided and the non-elided versions are equally acceptable, with neither sounding particularly "marked."

Lexicalization and grammaticalization 77

In contrast to English with restricted use of zero person forms and Chinese with more flexible uses, the Japanese language regularly adopts zero person forms in clauses of all types of mood structure. See the dialogue in Example 4.21.

Example 4.21 Zero person forms in Japanese

A: Φ Itsu   Nihon he   ki-mashi-ta-ka?
    when   Japan DIR   come-HON-PAST-INT
    "When did you come to Japan?"
B: Φ Senshuu ni   ki-mashi-ta.
    last week TMP   come-HON-PAST
    "I came last week."

It is totally acceptable and normal for Japanese to omit person forms in dialogues where the participant roles are self-evident and known to each party. It would sound very unnatural to put personal pronouns *anata* and *watashi* in the slots. Though speaker A may employ a nominal expression to refer to speaker B, as has been discussed in Section 4.1.2.3, it is extremely unlikely and almost never possible for speaker B to use any phonological person form to refer back to himself/herself.

Liu and Qiang (2009) classify zero person forms into three categories. The first type is shown in the above example from Japanese, where there is no explicit person expression but the zero form is seen neither as an ellipsis nor as non-standard usage. Instead, it is accepted as the usual, normal and customary identification of participant roles in discourse.

The second type of zero person form is found in many Indo-European languages where there is no explicit nominal or pronominal person expression but the verb is conjugated so that the participant role is manifest and can be readily interpreted judging from the personal marking integrated into the verb itself, as has been exemplified in Example 4.18.

The third type of zero person marker results from the lack of an explicit person form in the language system, hence the obligatoriness of a null in the clause. A notable example can be drawn from Old Chinese,[10] which lacks the third person nominative pronoun. The third person pronouns 其 and 厥 are used only in the genitive case, and 之 in the accusative case (Wang, 1980: 264). Consider Example 4.22, where the third person subject has to be left empty for lack of such a pronoun. If not empty, the opening must be filled with a full nominal expression, 子贡 (Zigong). The English translation below supplies the proper nominal.

Example 4.22 Zero person form for lack of a pronoun

子   谓   子贡   曰：
Confucius   say   Zigong PROJ
"女   与   回   也   孰   愈？"
you   and   Hui   TOP   who   superior

78 *Lexicalization and grammaticalization*

Φ 对	曰：	"赐 也	何	敢	望	回？
answer PROJ		Ci TOP	how dare	look over	Hui	
回	也	闻	一	以	知	十，
Hui	TOP	hear	one	so as to	know	ten
赐	也	闻	一	以	知	二。"
Ci	TOP	hear	one	so as to	know	two

(《论语·公冶长》)

"Confucius, speaking to Zigong, said, 'Who is superior? You or Hui?' Zigong answered, saying, 'How could I compare myself to Hui? He hears one point and understands the whole thing. I hear one point and understand a second one.'"

("Gongye Chang," *The Analects of Confucius*)[11]

Note in passing that in such a short excerpt from *The Analects of Confucius*, there are two interacting participants, namely Confucius and one of his disciples, Duanmu Ci (Zigong being a courtesy name), and a third participant that is not an interactant but merely referred to, Yan Hui, another disciple of Confucius's. However, the phonological person realizations in this piece of discourse vary according to their relations and social positions, and the relations between the compiler of the *Analects* and the participants involved, and may also be restricted by the linguistic properties of the grammatical system of Old Chinese. Table 4.3 provides a summary of the participant roles in Example 4.22. The motivation for proper choices among different kinds of Chinese names has been accounted for in Sections 4.1.2.2 and 4.1.2.3.

4.3 Personal pronouns

Personal pronouns in linguistics are pro-forms that substitute for nominal participant roles in discourse. Traditionally they are taken as referring to nouns or

Table 4.3 A summary of the participant roles in Example 4.22

Serial no.	Person form	Referring to...	By...	With...
1	子 (Confucius)	Confucius	compiler	honorific title
2	子贡 (Zigong)	Disciple 1	compiler	courtesy name
3	女 (you)	Disciple 1	Confucius	personal pronoun
4	回 (Hui)	Disciple 2	Confucius	given name
5	孰 (who)	unspecified	Confucius	interrogative pronoun
6	Φ	Disciple 1	compiler	zero form
7	赐 (Ci)	Disciple 1	Disciple 1	given name
8	回 (Hui)	Disciple 2	Disciple 1	given name
9	回 (Hui)	Disciple 2	Disciple 1	given name
10	赐 (Ci)	Disciple 2	Disciple 1	given name

nominal groups, but they differ from nominals in that they have distinctive morphological and syntactic properties. Personal pronouns, as one subcategory of pronouns, are classified as grammatical words, because they are a closed class and do not denote concrete lexical meanings. In the identification of and reference to participants in discourse, personal pronouns play a crucial role.

The notion of personal pronoun, however, makes up an issue of substantial dispute and controversy. If personal pronouns differ from nominal groups in their morphological, syntactic, semantic and interpretive properties, many Asian languages such as Thai and Japanese could be seen as being deficient in personal pronouns since such person forms manifest many properties of nominal groups. The notion of "pronoun" originally dates back to the Greek and Latin linguistic tradition (*pronomen*) and has since been adopted as a universal category for a class of words in the observation and analysis of natural languages. There has been an argument over whether this Latinate notion of pronoun should be applicable to non-Indo-European languages at all. For instance, the Japanese person expressions *watashi, anata*, etc. should not be treated as personal pronouns in the first place. On the other hand, a core feature of personal pronouns is their referential deficiency; that is, the identity of their referents is dependent on the linguistic or extralinguistic context. Judging from the inferability of such personal expressions, the Asian languages can be seen as not lacking personal pronouns.

Sugamoto (1989) voices a scalar approach to personal pronouns, in which the distinction between nouns and pronouns is rendered to be not discrete but gradable. Personal pronouns in some languages display more pronominal features, while those in other languages exhibit more nominal characteristics. She presents a pronominality scale where nominal and pronominal features form a continuum (shown in Figure 4.2) and suggests that Japanese personal pronouns display fewer pronominal characteristics than English ones do.

If personal pronouns in Chinese are brought into the picture, they are somewhere between Japanese and English personal pronouns; that is to say, Chinese

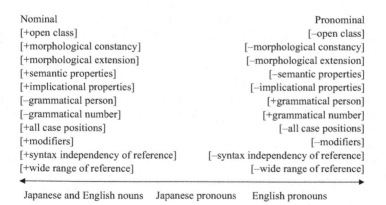

Figure 4.2 Nominal-pronominal continuum (after Sugamoto, 1989: 287)

personal pronouns possess more pronominal features than Japanese but fewer than English. The following is a brief comparison of personal pronouns across the three languages.

First, personal pronouns usually belong to a closed class in a paradigmatic set of a limited number of words. In English, there is basically one pronoun for each grammatical person, number and case variety. This is also true in the case of modern Chinese. In classic Chinese, there are more members for each grammatical person, e.g. 吾, 我, 余, 予, etc. for the first person singular; 汝, 尔, 若, 乃, etc. for the second person singular. The multiplicity of Japanese personal pronouns is also well known, such as *watashi, watakushi, boku, ore, ware*, etc. for the first person singular and *anata, kimi, omae, kisama*, etc. for the second person singular.

Second, pronouns tend to be inconstant in morphological form and not to take morphological extensions. This is true in English in that suppletive forms are used to indicate different numbers and cases, e.g. *I/we/me/my*. However, personal pronouns in Chinese and Japanese do not resort to suppletion but form the plural or possessive by taking the same affix as nominal groups would, e.g. 我/我们/我的 and *watashi/watashi-tachi/watashi-no*. While Chinese has no accusative case ending, Japanese employs the same postpositional participle *wo* for the accusative case for both nouns and pronouns.

Third, pronouns generally do not contain specific semantic content, but their primary function is to refer to participants in discourse and convey the grammatical features associated with them. Their experiential meaning is strictly determined by their referential interpretation. In opposition, the primary function of nominals is to name the participants instead of merely referring to them. Nominals have high degrees of semantic specificity. In contrast, the semantic content of pronouns is confined to broad features only. In English and Chinese, the pronominal feature is prominent; for example, the first person singular pronouns *I* and 我 have only the semantic features of [+animate, +human]. In contrast, in Japanese, some personal pronouns may display more nominal features; for example, the first person singular pronoun *boku* has semantic features of [+animate, +human, +male]. Thus, Japanese personal pronouns again stand slightly closer to the nominal side along the pronominality scale as far as semantic properties are concerned.

Fourth, personal pronouns tend not to vary stylistically and sociolinguistically, but nominal groups might. For example, *father, dad, daddy* and *the old man* show different degrees of intimacy and are used on different occasions. Personal pronouns in English do not exhibit variable stylistic and sociolinguistic implications, with items like *I* or *you* applicable to diverse social settings. Chinese pronouns move a bit toward the nominal side, with some personal pronouns indicating respect and formality, such as the honorific second person pronoun 您 in contrast to the casual form 你. Japanese personal pronouns are more complicated in terms of social and stylistic implications; for example, the first person singular pronoun *watakushi* implies a sense of humbleness, *boku* is typically used by young male people in an informal situation, and *ore* is still more casual and arrogant-sounding and is almost exclusively used by a male speaker addressing someone he feels really close to. These social and stylistic implications in most cases result

Lexicalization and grammaticalization 81

from "direct or indirect consequences of the words' original nominal meanings" (Sugamoto, 1989: 273). Therefore, the Japanese pronouns are still not fully pronominalized, and so they are found farther from the pronominal end of the pronominality cline than Chinese pronouns, and yet farther from English pronouns.

Fifth, as for grammatical persons, the pronouns in English, Chinese and Japanese are similar in that they all distinguish among the first, second and third person, while nominals are in most cases third person. Grammatical number is also a referential property of pronouns: as discussed above, number in English pronouns is indicated by suppletive forms, while for Chinese and Japanese personal pronouns number is indicated by plural suffixes.

The sixth benchmark to measure pronominality is the ability to take modifiers. English personal pronouns may take modifiers under very restricted circumstances: the accusative forms of pronouns may be preceded by certain adjectives of judgment used in exclamations, e.g. Example 4.23(a) and (b). Sometimes pronouns can take determiners, e.g. Example 4.23(c) and (d), but such occasions are not applicable to all contexts. Pronouns do not normally take determiners (Example 4.23(e)), demonstratives (Example 4.23(f)) or possessives (Example 4.23(g)).

Example 4.23 English pronouns with modifiers

(a) Poor **me**!
(b) Lucky **you**!
(c) That was not the real **me**.
(d) It's a **she**! (not a male)
(e) *the **he**
(f) *those **them**
(g) *your **her**

In Chinese, the restrictions are less tight, resulting in more possibilities for personal pronouns to take modifiers. Examples are provided in Example 4.24(a)–(c). However, pronouns in Chinese still cannot combine freely with modifiers; normally, pronouns do not follow demonstratives (at least not for plural pronouns) (Example 4.24(d) and (e)) or possessives (Example 4.24(f)).

Example 4.24 Chinese pronouns with modifiers

(a) 可怜的　　**他**
    poor　　　him
(b) 我　已经　不　是　十年前　　的　　**我**　了。
    I　already　NEG　be　ten years ago　GEN　me　PERF
(c) 此刻　　　的　**你**，是否　会　想念　当时　　的　**她**?
    this moment　GEN　you　whether　will　miss　that time　GEN　her
(d) ?那个　**她**
    that　　her
(e) *这些　**我们**
    these　us

82 *Lexicalization and grammaticalization*

(f) ?我的　他
　　my　　him

Closer to the nominal extreme, Japanese pronouns allow a great range of modifications. They can be modified by demonstratives, possessives, any adjectives or even embedded clauses. Consider Example 4.25.

Example 4.25 Japanese pronouns with modifiers

(a) kono **kare**
　　this　he
(b) watashi no　　**anata**
　　I GEN (my)　　you
(c) yasashii　**kanojo**
　　gentle　　she
(d) sensei ni　　home-rare-ta　　**watashi**
　　teacher AGT　praise-PASS-PAST　I
　　"?I, who was praised by the teacher"

With regard to the above account, the major characteristics of the pronominal end as representative of personal pronouns can be summed up as follows:

(1) closed class
(2) morphological inconstancy
(3) deficiency in specific semantic content
(4) lack of stylistic and sociolinguistic implications
(5) grammatical person and number
(6) restricted ability to take modifiers

Thus, as far as personal pronouns in English, Chinese and Japanese are concerned, they are located at different positions along the nominal-pronominal scale, as is roughly shown in Figure 4.3.

Typological studies may find the personal pronouns in different languages fitting into different spots along the above cline (for Thai and Polish see Siewierska, 2004: 9–13), hence the complexity of personal pronouns and their idiosyncratic performances in discourse. Although the notion of personal pronouns can be taken as universal, their distinctive features across languages are not to be neglected.

Figure 4.3 English/Chinese/Japanese pronouns on the pronominality scale

4.4 Chapter summary

In this chapter, the two major means of realization of participant roles in discourse, i.e. lexicalization and grammaticalization, are explored. Lexicalization of person means that information related to participants in discourse can be made available through lexical items denoting names of entities, processes and qualities. The most relevant lexical means identifying and referring to participant roles in discourse would intuitively seem to be – as it indeed is – names of entities, that is, nouns or nominal groups in general, for the obvious reason that participants in discourse are by nature entities. What is more, such entities, when identified with nominals, are for the most part third person, because they are referred to rather than being directly involved in any interacting locution. However, many examples have been shown to suggest that, under certain circumstances, nominal groups can be employed to refer to either the addresser (first person) or the addressee (second person). With such usages, there is inevitably an interpersonally loaded meaning conveyed in the discourse, embodying stylistic or sociolinguistic nuances, such as formality, respect, power relations, solidarity, intimacy, etc.

Person-related meaning is also likely to be lexicalized with verbs, which, even if uninflected, may be evident in clarifying participant roles in discourse. Such verbs are especially possible in languages that reflect societies with strict social class orders or hierarchies, such as Japanese. In such languages, careful choices have to be made among the reservoir of verbs with the same experiential meaning in accordance with the social statuses of the address and the addressee, how close they are to each other and how formal they sense their language needs to be.

Qualities and circumstances in discourse seem to be the least likely indicator of participant roles; however, the meaning potential of human language does allow the identification of person to be incarnated in adjectives and adverbs. The denotation of person is simply everywhere in lexical words.

This also holds true for grammatical means. Personal pronouns, as the most prominent grammatical means for indicating participant roles in discourse, themselves manifest different tendencies along the nominal-pronominal continuum across languages. They can be seen as being situated on the borderline between purely lexical and purely grammatical means of indicating person.

A step further toward the grammatical end of person reference are clitics, "elements with some of the properties characteristic of words and some characteristic of affixes" (Zwicky, 1994: xii). Typologically, in terms of clitics of person, there are pure clitics, clitics that look like affixes and also clitics that look like independent pronouns. Therefore, clitics, in turn, can be regarded as the borderline between independent personal pronouns and affixes.

Suffixes of inflectional morphology are a powerful grammatical means of indicating person in many languages in the world. The verb conjugations of Indo-European languages are evident examples of this point, including the third person relic *-s* in Modern English. Such inflectional suffixes of person go as far as obviating the necessity of explicit nominal or pronominal person markers in some languages (such as Spanish and Italian), while some make the subjective personal pronouns somewhat redundant and move them into the category of clitics (such as French).

At the extreme of grammatical means, the absence of phonological form as a person marker may be found in many circumstances as well. When information about the referent is easily accessible in the context, the explicit form of coding might become unnecessary. Or there is not any person marker available in a certain paradigm of person forms, such as the third person singular nominative pronoun in Old Chinese and the third person subject agreement prefixes in Seri, a Mexican language, reported by Marlett (1990: 514).

When all the aspects addressed in this chapter are taken into account, the lexical and grammatical means of expressing the concept of person can be summarized with a cline, too, starting from lexical items and developing all the way to the grammatical pole.

lexical items > independent pronouns > clitics > affixes > zero forms

This cline is particularly significant in accounting for the complementarity between lexis and grammar, an essential feature of human beings' construal of their experience of the world. This point will be elaborated on in the next chapter.

Notes

1 Translated by James Legge.
2 Translated by C. H. Brewitt-Taylor.
3 Note that the translations provided in parentheses are strictly literal so as to show the original meaning of the individual words. In usual practice when translating actual texts, such humble terms are often rendered into English differently, e.g. 鄙人: *my humble self, your humble servant, I, me*, etc.
4 A pop singer from Taiwan.
5 The author is indebted to Professor J. R. Martin for asking Assistant Professor C.A.M. Gouveia for his 34th International Systemic Functional Congress (ISFC) presentation slides and sending them to the author.
6 Translated by James Legge.
7 Translated by Zhang Peiji.
8 This term is translated literally from *pronombre objetivo* in Spanish.
9 See http://en.wiktionary.org/wiki/consigo.
10 Old Chinese (上古汉语), also known as Archaic Chinese, refers to the Chinese language from the initial stage of written records (circa 1200 B.C.) until the 3rd century B.C.
11 Translated by A. Charles Muller.

5 Complementarity between lexis and grammar
A systemic functional perspective

Grammatical models and theories arising around the middle of the 20th century have largely detached and abstracted themselves from the actual performances of language, following the Chomskyan practice. Such a practice advocates language competence as comprising a "lexicon" and a set of "generative rules." Traditional studies of language, too, conceive of language as working through a "vocabulary" and a "grammar." In contrast to these linguistic conceptions, Systemic Functional Linguistics (SFL) prioritizes meaning (semantics/discourse semantics) as the starting and focal point of analysis. Meaning is realized by lexicogrammar, which incorporates both lexis and grammar, and the two form a relation of complementarity. Meaning can be realized and linguistic analysis can be carried out through either the lexical or the grammatical gateway. Therefore, SFL can better serve the job of analyzing the functioning of language, including Chinese (Cheng, 1993: 165).

This chapter is intended to provide an account for the complementarity between lexis and grammar in their construal of meaning in relation to the system of person. The first section addresses SFL's long-standing position on complementarities in language and in ways of linguistic analysis. The second section is dedicated specifically to the complementarity between lexis and grammar, and the third section recalls the manifestation of this type of complementarity with respect to the person system. The fourth section provides a typological account from the SFL perspective and examines how the movement of person marking forms along the lexis-grammar cline across languages reflects the diversified resources and motifs in the construal of the same meaning, i.e. meaning related to the person system.

5.1 An overview of complementarity in SFL

5.1.1 The term "complementarity"

Complementarity is a relationship in which two or more things enhance or emphasize each other's qualities or properties and together form a balanced entirety. The term "complementary" is widely used in scientific literature. For example, in mathematics, two angles are said to be complementary if they sum up to 90 degrees; "complementary colors" refers to pairs of colors that are of opposite hue and give white when combined, such as red and green.

86 *Complementarity between lexis and grammar*

What is particularly relevant to complementarity in SFL is the wave-particle duality in quantum theory in physics, where light or radiation has the behavior of either waves or particles, depending on the circumstances of the experiment. Such a duality gives rise to the principle of complementarity, which suggests that some objects have dual properties that appear to be contradictory because normally the two sides are mutually exclusive; however, both of them are possible. It is usually not likely that one will observe both at the same time though they exist simultaneously. For one single phenomenon, it can be measured either way, but not at the same time, and the same measurement cannot apply to both.

5.1.2 Complementarities in language

Apart from the natural sciences, the principle of complementarities is found in the study of language, too. For example, the noun *language* can be seen as either a mass noun or a count noun, seemingly contradictory but both feasible. When it is used as a mass noun, e.g. *complementarities in language*, here *language* refers to the abstract semiotic system, without any preceding determiner or plurality ending. When it is used to mean a particular kind of language, e.g. *Chinese is a difficult language*, it is a count noun. The two interpretations cannot stand at the same time but are equally reasonable depending on the situation.

In terms of semantic space, some domains of human experience can be construed in two contradictory ways, as in pairs like *like* vs. *please*, *believe* vs. *convince*, *fear* vs. *frighten*, *enjoy* vs. *delight*, etc. Each alternative of the pairs is dependent on the angle by which the same phenomenon is observed.

According to Halliday (2008: 33), complementarity is "a fundamental property of language," and the two terms in the complementary dyads of language are "pairs of opposites that are exclusive, and even contradictory, but such that both are involved in every manifestation of language."

Halliday (2008), on the basis of his three lectures at Birmingham University, the University of Liverpool and the University of Nottingham, summarizes three basic complementarities in language, including those between lexis and grammar, language as system and language as text, and the two modes of writing and speaking.

The complementarity between lexis and grammar, as the key issue of this book, is the basis for the idea of lexicogrammar as a single unified stratum. The second type of complementarity emphasizes the fact that system and text are two aspects of a single phenomenon – language. They are not two separate orders of reality, although they tend to be treated as if they were. The system determines the meaning and *valeur* of choices actually made by speakers, while the text is an instantiation of the system, a process and product of making selections within the meaning potential. The third type of complementarity, i.e. that between speaking and writing, is exhibited through their respective strategies for organizing meaning and their respective ways of achieving and managing complexity. Written language tends to be lexically dense but grammatically simple, packaging meaning into highly condensed structures; spoken language tends to be grammatically intricate but lexically sparse, knotting together long and transparent clauses into intricate patterns of logico-semantic relationship.

5.1.3 Complementarities in SFL metalanguage

The idea of complementarity in SFL can be traced back to its initial stage of development and holds a prominent place in its theoretical modeling of language (see Halliday, 1961, 1985a/1994, 1987, 1992a, 1995, 1997). Many SFL approaches to the observation and interpretation of language are conducted by virtue of complementarities, "models deriving from alternative perspectives which contradict each other and yet are both 'true'" (Halliday, 1997: 21). The following are some demonstrations of such complementary approaches.

5.1.3.1 Metafunction

The basic functions of language in the environment of ecological and social settings, which are intrinsic to language, are called metafunctions by the SFL School. The metafunctions are an integral part of SFL theories, and language has evolved along with these functions in the human species. A lot of the introductory SFL literature explains in detail what the metafunctions are (see Halliday, 1985a/1994; Halliday & Matthiessen, 2004; Matthiessen & Halliday, 2009; etc.).

The construal of human experience, such as naming things, processes and qualities, and configuring the different elements into complex patterns, is referred to as ideational metafunction, which consists of two components, the experiential function and the logical function. Language is also used to enact the language users' social and personal relationships with other people around them. The lexicogrammatical resources of language can create or identify propositions and proposals through systems of MOOD and MODALITY, and express appraisal of people and things that are being talked about. This function is known as interpersonal metafunction. The third metafunction is related to the construction of text via linguistic resources, i.e. textual metafunction. It facilitates the building of a discursive structure, the organization of information flow and the generation of cohesion and continuity in the text.

The three components are conceived of as functioning simultaneously and form a relation of complementarity between one another (Figure 5.1). The three broad areas of metafunctions set out to explain how language resources are organized to make meaning and are functionally bound to meaning.

5.1.3.2 Axis

The complementary dimensions of system and structure in SFL are referred to as axis (Martin & Rose, 2008: 23). SFL foregrounds language as meaning potential, i.e. options for meaning. The paradigmatic relationship among linguistic elements is viewed by SFL as one of choices as resources for making meaning, hence the systemic component in SFL. System is the ordering on the paradigmatic axis: "patterns in what *could go instead of* what" (Halliday & Matthiessen, 2004: 22).

Structure, on the other hand, is the syntagmatic ordering of language along the other axis: "what *goes together with* what" (ibid.). Although the systemic (paradigmatic) relations are prominent in SFL, any feature in any system is realized

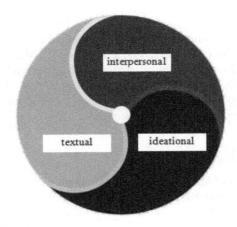

Figure 5.1 Complementarity of metafunctions

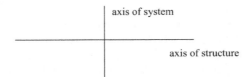

Figure 5.2 Complementarity of axis

through a certain kind of syntagmatic structure. In other words, choices from system networks are realized as functional elements of structure.

The essential connection between system (paradigmatic choice) and structure (syntagmatic realization) can be illustrated in a system network with realizations (refer back to Figure 2.2 in Chapter Two for an instance concerning the English MOOD system). It is also a relationship of complementarity in that the system contributes to the formation of structure, and the structure, in turn, reflects the functional organization of the system (Figure 5.2).

5.1.3.3 Agnation

Systemic theory of language is about what options are available to language users, how these options are realized and how they are related. This relation is called agnation (Martin & Matthiessen, 1991). The notation of system networks constitutes a typological theory of language, in which the way options form systems is made explicit. Systemic typology stands as a powerful tool of interpreting agnation; however, there is a complementary perspective on agnation – topology – which can account for agnations that are difficult to represent in a satisfactorily clear-cut way.

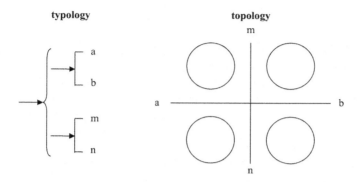

Figure 5.3 Complementarity of agnation

Typological description of linguistic phenomena sometimes comes across problems and therefore has its limitations. The best acknowledged example would be the description of vowels: the descriptive features of vowels are not so conveniently divided into such simple terms as high/middle/low or front/central/back. On most occasions the features of vowels are not this clear-cut. Thus, a topological orientation would be more helpful. A topological approach establishes a set of criteria for determining the degree of proximity of a certain linguistic phenomenon among members of the same category, and solves quandaries that might show up in devising system networks. Figure 5.3 demonstrates how typological and topological strategies work and complement each other.

The complementarity between typology and topology is particularly relevant to the present study in that topological approaches are helpful in working with a variety of languages, i.e. language typology. Such studies have long been haunted by troubles in setting up distinct categories universally applicable to different languages (see Martin, 1983). For the combination of the two orientations in discourse analysis, see Lemke (1999).

5.1.3.4 *Perspective*

Language as meaning potential can be seen from two complementary perspectives: the potential seen from the static perspective is called a synoptic system, and it is called a dynamic system when viewed actively. Texts are generated from static systems, while processes are generated from dynamic systems (Martin, 1985: 258).

According to Martin (1985), most works of linguists following the Saussurean tradition have been dominated by synoptic perspectives; however, when it comes to text structure, it needs to be emphasized that texts are dynamic processes taking place in time. For example, a system network representing a genre potential, e.g. a service encounter, illustrates the synoptic perspective, while the flowchart notation of the same genre potential is known as a dynamic perspective (see Ventola, 1987: 70–76).

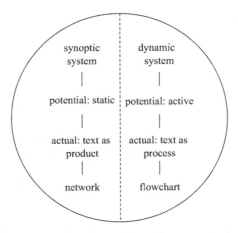

Figure 5.4 Complementarity of perspective

As indicated above, the complementarity between the synoptic and dynamic perspectives is particularly applicable to genre studies. Synoptic generic system networks can capture the generic choices in the situation of culture and define generic features of text as a product; however, static system networks do not specify sequence or the chronological unfolding of the text as a process. This is exactly where the dynamic perspective fits in. Dynamic flowcharts represent the potential of text linearization and the process in which interactants negotiate meaning and create texts over time. The complementary relationship between the static and active approaches is exhibited in Figure 5.4.

5.1.3.5 Semogenesis

The process in which human beings create meaning through human language is called semogenesis (Halliday & Matthiessen, 1999: 17). Three types of semogenic processes are recognized by SFL, namely logogenesis, ontogenesis and phylogenesis. This "evolutionary theory of meaning" was first put forward in Halliday (1992a).

Logogenesis refers to the unfolding of the text, or the act of meaning. The potential for creating meaning is constantly adjusted in accordance with what has gone before, with choices opened up or restricted for what is to follow. Ontogenesis refers to the development of the individual user of language. Phylogenesis refers to the evolution of human language as a whole, or "the genealogy of the culture" (Martin & McCormack, 2001: 15).

The three types of semogenic processes are complementary in that, on the one hand, logogenesis provides material for ontogenesis, which in turn provides material for phylogenesis; and, on the other hand, phylogenesis provides an environment for ontogenesis, which in turn provides an environment for logogenesis. That is to say, instances of text construct individual speakers' meaning potential, which in turn constructs the meaning potential of the species; the system of language of the species provides the environment for the emergence of individuals' meaning potential, which in turn provides the environment for the creation of the meaning of texts. This relationship of complementarity is outlined in Figure 5.5.

From Sections 5.1.2 and 5.1.3, it is apparent that the systemic functional theory adopts a viewpoint based on the idea of complementarity not only for language as the object of study and analysis but also for metalanguage as the approach to achieve these ends. The SFL metalinguistic resources are systemically summarized in Figure 5.6.

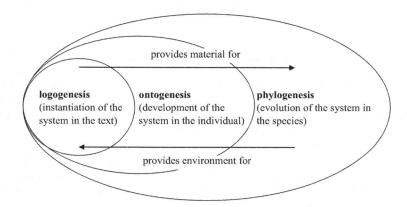

Figure 5.5 Complementarity of semogenesis (combining Halliday & Matthiessen, 1999: 18 and Martin & McCormack, 2001: 15)

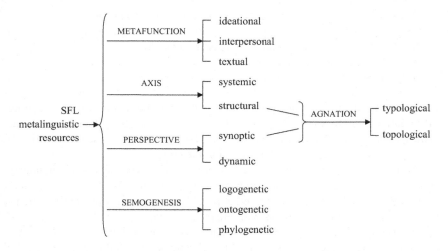

Figure 5.6 SFL metalinguistic resources (adapted and revised from Martin & Matthiessen, 1991: 361)

The integration of two (or more) mutually dependent and defining properties of language or metalanguage is largely comparable to the traditional Chinese yin-yang philosophy, with ostensibly incompatible aspects coexistent in unified harmony. The comparability of the semogenic process and Chinese yin-yang philosophy is presented in Halliday and Matthiessen (1999: 19–23) and elaborated on in Yan (2010).[1]

As Yan (2010) points out, language is used to construe one's experience of the world, which is in turn constructed by language. The two aspects are both mutually distinctive and interactive. So are the various complementary facets in language and the approaches to its interpretation. With this insight emphasized, the next section of this chapter will address the complementarity between lexis and grammar and its application specifically to the system of person.

5.2 Complementarity between lexis and grammar

SFL holds that human language develops epigenetically in a definable sequence, beginning with the non-stratified pairing of meaning and sound as protolanguage and later moving to higher order consciousness around the second year of life, when the stratum of lexicogrammar appears (Halliday, 1975).

Lexis and grammar form a single unified stratum along a continuum, or cline; they are complementary most prominently in their ideational function. That is to say, any phenomenon of human experience can be construed either way: either lexically or grammatically. And each brings its own contribution to the meaning of the whole. Consider Example 5.1.

Example 5.1 Lexis-grammar complementarity in polarity (Wang, 2010: 21)

(a1) In some areas girls are not allowed to go to school.
(a2) In some areas girls are denied their rights to go to school.
(b1) The president didn't approve of a tax increase on gasoline.
(b2) The president vetoed a tax increase on gasoline.
(c1) We won't accept this offer.
(c2) We will refuse this offer.

In construing meaning of negative polarity, the grammatical means of attaching the negative operator *not* to the Finite element of the clause can be resorted to, as is the case in (a1), (b1) and (c1), while lexical words are used in (a2), (b2) and (c2) to equally achieve the construal of the same meaning.

Halliday (2008) draws an analogy between lexis-grammar complementarity and particle-wave duality in quantum mechanics, previously mentioned in Section 5.1.1. Lexical items are compared to particles because they are specific members that construe phenomena as particulars; grammatical systems are compared to waves since they are general terms that construe experiences as generalities. For a lexicologist, the ideal outcome of linguistic study would be to extend the lexicological method to the grammar end and to reduce all the grammatical rules to a part of lexis, with grammatical words such as *not, and, to* and *if* entered and defined in the dictionary. On the other hand, for a grammarian, his or her dream would be to turn the whole of linguistic form into grammar and to show that lexis can be defined as the "most delicate grammar" (see Hasan, 1987). The complementarity between lexis and grammar is summarized in Figure 5.7.

As regards this complementarity, there are several key issues that are worth paying due attention to. First, since lexis and grammar are two ends of a cline, with no clear boundary in between, naturally there might be some fuzzy areas in the middle of the cline where complex systems are located which are difficult to explain. Halliday (2008: 26–27) provides examples of *overlook* and *see through*: they can be either

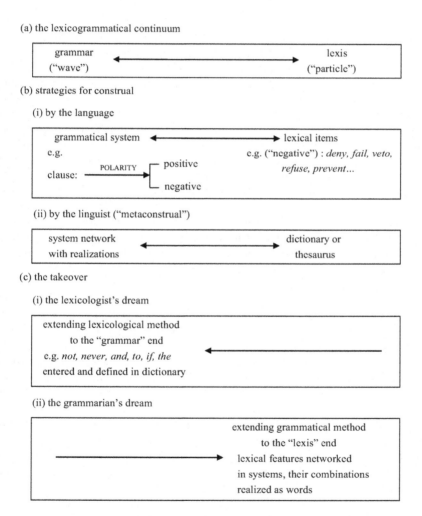

Figure 5.7 Complementarity between lexis and grammar (Halliday, 2008: 33)

approached by lexical means—that is, they can be looked up in a dictionary which provides definitions—or described in a grammar book which treats *overlook* as a derivational compound made up of the prefix *over-* plus a verb of perception, and *see through* as a verbal phrase consisting of a main verb and a preposition/adverb.

This fuzziness and complexity can be illustrated with instances from a wide range of other languages as well. In Chinese, the word 打倒 (to knock down, overthrow) can either be seen as a separate lexical item or be conceived of as grammatically compounded from the verb 打 (to knock) plus the complement element 倒 (down), which functions as the completive/resultative phase of the action. In Japanese, the word *iyagaru* (to dislike) can be found in a dictionary as a lexical entry or recognized grammatically by separating the derivational morpheme *-garu* as suffixed to the adnominal form of an adjective base. In French, *se laver* (to wash) can be lexically defined as the infinitive form of a reflexive verb, or alternatively analyzed by grammatical means with *se* regarded as a clitic. In German, the verb *ankommen* (to arrive) is by all means a lexical word while at the same time *an-* is picked out as a grammatical prefix indicating motion or direction preceding the verb root *kommen* (to come).

Each of the above phenomena can be looked at either way. They can be interpreted lexically, as lexical items or collocations, or grammatically, as grammatical structures and classes. The two ways present different images of the whole; however, it is still the same phenomenon that is being construed and interpreted.

Second, a single cline for the lexicogrammatical stratum may result in the same meaning being construed by different methods in different languages and thus ending up in different locations along the cline. If a cross-language comparison is made between English and Chinese, it can be found out that, in most cases, the two languages situate the various semantic domains at roughly equivalent locations along the lexicogrammatical continuum. For example, experiential categories of entities, processes and qualities are generally lexical, while mood, modality and logical meanings are mostly construed grammatically.

Nonetheless, there are still some noticeable disparities between the two languages in terms of construal of experiential meaning. Halliday and Matthiessen (1999: 299–300) report two significant areas of such disparity. First, the Chinese language treats the phase of a process more grammatically than English does, by realizing the completive phase or directional phase with a closed set of postpositive verbs; second, tense in Chinese is construed much less grammatically than in English in that it is realized by "time adverbs" instead of inflectional morphology. A synopsis and examples are given in Table 5.1.

Third, meanings on the lexicogrammatical continuum are ready to migrate along this cline. This migration may be synchronic, when the same meaning is construed by different means, some more lexical and others more grammatical, in a single language or across various languages, as illustrated above; the movement can also be diachronic if the evolution of realizations of a certain meaning is considered. For example, the colloquial *let's* used as an introductory particle in some varieties of English has shifted from a lexical set to a grammatical unit, expressing a meaning of urging or encouraging (Example 5.2).

Table 5.1 Disparities in locations on the lexis-grammar continuum

	Chinese	English
(1) phase of Process	grammatical e.g. 分-分出	lexical e.g. *separate-distinguish*
(2) tense	lexical e.g. 去年, 马上, 已经 "last year, at once, already"	grammatical e.g. *walked, will drive*

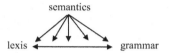

Figure 5.8 Relexicogrammaticalization (after Halliday, 2008: 176)

Example 5.2 Grammatical *let's* (Hopper & Traugott, 1993: 11)

(a) **Let's** you and him fight.
(b) **Let's** you go first, then if we have any money left I'll go.

In terms of direction, the migration can take place toward either the grammatical or the lexical end, termed "grammaticalization" and "lexicalization" from the perspective of phylogenesis. It should once again be emphasized that this move from lexis to grammar, or the other way round, is not a jump across ranks, but an alteration of the degree of delicacy. Figure 5.8 shows the relationship between meaning and wording, adopting a "from above" approach, and also illustrates the idea of "relexicogrammaticalization."

5.3 Lexis-grammar complementarity in the system of person

5.3.1 *Participant accessibility in discourse*

As was stated above, the complementarity between lexis and grammar, according to SFL, is most prominent in the ideational metafunction. When it comes to the system of person, its ideational function is mainly performed in the identification of and reference to the participants in the clause. The specific expressions of person chosen by the addresser along the lexicogrammatical continuum reflect how he or she judges the accessibility of the particular entities for the addressee. The addresser chooses a person form with high mental accessibility to the entity (more toward the grammatical end) when the information about this participant is not so difficult for the addressee to retrieve in the current phase of discourse. Likewise, when the information about the participant needs to be more specifically provided, the addresser would select a less attenuated form (more toward the lexical end). All the choices come from the vast reservoir of meaning potential that language has to provide, either lexically or grammatically, for the construal of ideational meaning.

Ariel (2000) develops a discourse referent accessibility marking scale which is quite representative of many languages, though she also acknowledges that the form-function correlation between those markers and mental accessibility is not perfectly transparent.

The accessibility marking scale

zero < reflexives < poor agreement markers < rich agreement markers < reduced/cliticized pronouns < unstressed pronouns < stressed pronouns < stressed pronouns + gesture < proximal demonstrative (+NP) < distal demonstrative (+NP) < proximal demonstrative (+NP) + modifier < distal demonstrative (+NP) + modifier < first name < last name < short definite description < long definite description < full name < full name + modifier

(Ariel, 2000: 205)

It is apparent enough that the accessibility scale devised by Ariel essentially corresponds to the cline of person extending from the grammar end to the lexis end which was developed in the previous chapter, although it is more human-based, which could be seen as a subset of the notion of participant in this study. "Participant" in this book refers to any human or non-human entity in a discourse.

5.3.2 Metafunction

Ideationally, the system of person in language functions to construe meaning related to participant roles, an important aspect of human experience of the world. Similar to many things in the human world whose meaning needs to be construed through language, the manifestations of the system of person are complex and diverse. On the one hand, participating entities in discourse can be sorted out as particular things that have distinctive signifiers which give the participants a specific class and value. Under these circumstances lexical means are employed to achieve the construal of person-related meanings. On the other hand, meanings concerning participant roles can have certain general characteristics and properties which are abstracted from the particularities and are therefore construed as general features through grammatical means. All the complexities of the system of person as accounted for in Chapter Three demand the two seemingly contrastive perspectives on construal: the lexical perspective is specific and open, and demands less effort in accessing and retrieving participant information; the grammatical perspective is general and closed, and provides higher accessibility and retrievability of the same phenomenon.

Besides construing experience of the world, human language also functions interpersonally in enacting relationships among one another. It is more than self-evident that the system of "person" plays a part in fulfilling an interpersonal function. The realization of speech functions (statement, question, command and offer) is inextricably relevant to person roles in discourse; choices and

Complementarity between lexis and grammar 97

positions of person forms in discourse also have much to do with mood, modality and appraisal. Again, the same two perspectives join hands in this area. Different choices of person forms made along the lexis-grammar continuum represent different ways of enacting and managing different human relationships.

To weave the ideational and interpersonal functions together, language evolves the textual metafunction, which enables language itself to be organized in the form of discourse. Textually, lexical and grammatical person forms may achieve different degrees of thematic prominence and/or Given/New status. Usually, the lexical person forms contain more New information and tend to be given more thematic prominence, whereas grammatical person forms are more likely to be known information and function as a certain kind of cohesive device that facilitates the management of meaning in the discourse.

5.3.3 *Grammaticalization revisited*

Three key issues regarding lexis-grammar complementarity were pointed out in Section 5.2: i.e. (1) some complicated phenomena are hard to explain in terms of lexical or grammatical means of construal; (2) there may be cross-language differences in lexical and grammatical construal of the same meaning; and (3) the same meaning may migrate to different locations along the lexis-grammar continuum. They apply to the system of person, too. The first issue has been accounted for at length in the previous chapter (Section 4.3), where personal pronouns were described and interpreted as a complex class displaying different degrees of lexical or grammatical features on various occasions. The second issue is also prevalent in the previous chapter, with many examples drawn from an assortment of languages, and this issue will be picked up again in the next section. The third issue, when it comes to person, remains unaddressed so far with regard to diachronic movement. Person meanings characteristically move over time from the lexis end to the grammar end, a process termed "grammaticalization."

Grammatical person markers, including personal pronouns, clitics, inflectional affixes and zero forms, belong to one of the most stable parts of language; however, they are subject to change as well. These person markers are seen as originating from lexical items, just as other grammatical items often begin their life as regular lexical items (Meillet, 1912). From a lexical item to a grammatical marker, a certain person form goes through a series of changes in phonology, morphology, syntax and semantics. Phonologically, the item undergoes reduction in sound, resulting in simpler pronunciation; morphologically, it loses independent word status through cliticization and affixation; syntactically, the position of the item becomes fossilized; and, semantically, it drops full semantic content and assumes a more abstract and general meaning.

Some expressions used to denote person are transparently related to, or even homophonous with, nominals expressing various types of human relationships, kinship or titles, although the lexical origins or person markers are mostly buried in history (Siewierska, 2004: 247). It is reported that in many Southeast Asian languages, such as Thai, Vietnamese, Bahasa Malay, etc., the link between personal pronouns (if they are seen as existing in such languages) and lexical items is patently obvious. Person forms used to refer to the first person tend to be related to nominal groups of belittlement, such as *slave, servant*, etc. Those for the second person tend to be concerned with lexical expressions of honorification and aggrandizement, such as *lord, master*, etc.

The Japanese language provides more familiar examples concerning this point. The first person pronoun *boku* (with kanji 僕) originally meant "servant" or "slave" when it was borrowed from Chinese, but it has now grammaticalized into a personal pronoun with no more such humbleness. The second person pronoun *kimi* (with kanji 君) is also loaned from Chinese, originally meaning "king"; however, it has gradually lost the lexical semantic content and was reduced to a personal pronoun to address someone with a high social status, before it went further to another extreme, i.e. to address a listener with a lower status than the speaker.

Apart from nominal groups denoting human relationships and terms of belittlement and aggrandizement, some personal pronouns in some languages may stem from other things. Take, for example, the second person honorific pronoun in Korean, *dangsin*, which is a Korean-coined word with Chinese lexical roots *dang* (當) and *sin* (身). It is obvious that the pronoun derives from full lexical expression meaning "the body present at the time and place of speaking." The first person singular pronoun 我 in Chinese comes from a lexical origin, too. It originates from the full lexical item meaning "halberd" – a battle weapon combining an axe and a spear with a long shaft. Such a meaning is reflected in the old graphology – oracle bone script, too, which looks like 丮. It gradually migrates toward the grammatical end and loses its lexical denotation, following this process:

halberd→holding a halberd→referring to oneself as halberd holder
→1st person

Once grammaticalized into a personal pronoun, the person marker might continue moving along the lexis-grammar continuum further to the grammar end, and it reduces to a clitic, a bound morpheme or ultimately a zero form. Previous studies indicate that typologists have arrived at a consensus that most clitics and verbal inflections result from gradual development of pronouns (see Greenberg, 1966; Givón, 1976; Steele, 1977; Dixon, 1979, 1980; Comrie, 1981; Bosch, 1983; Lehmann, 1987; Hopper & Traugott, 1993; Ariel, 2000).

However, the movement of personal forms from lexical items to pronouns and further to clitics and affixes cannot take place simultaneously for different persons, numbers or genders, or among different languages. Intermediate states, such as the unclear boundary between nominal and pronominal features of pronouns, or between clitics and affixes, reflect the changes in progress. Nonetheless, in each stage of the development there is a comparatively stable system from which person-related choices can potentially be made. Consider the different stages of grammaticalization of person forms in French and Spanish: in a typical French declarative clause, an inflected verb needs to be preceded by a nominal group, or a personal pronoun which is deemed as clitic-like, whereas in Spanish the conjugated verb can make an explicit subject entirely unnecessary.

Complementarity between lexis and grammar 99

Interestingly, what might add to the universality of person's turning up at different locations along the lexis-grammar cline is the simultaneous existence of different "personal pronouns" found in languages as old as Egyptian (before it went extinct). In Egyptian grammar, personal pronouns may take three different forms, i.e. independent pronouns, dependent pronouns and suffix pronouns (see Gardiner, 1957). Therefore, for a simple example, the clause *thou art in the house* might be realized in Egyptian with three possibilities:

Example 5.3 Egyptian personal pronouns (hieroglyphs with transcription)

(a) **ntk** m pr (independent pronoun)[2]

(b) mk **Tw** m pr (dependent pronoun)
behold you in house

(c) jw=k m pr (suffix pronoun)[3]
be=you in house

Note that the term "dependent pronoun" actually refers to what is accepted linguistically as a "clitic" since it is, by definition, "less closely attached to a preceding word than the suffix pronouns, but can never stand as first word of a sentence" (Gardiner, 1957: 42). What is called a "suffix pronoun" is by all means an inflectional morpheme which lies further to the grammar extreme of the cline in question. The same experiential meaning is realized by three different possibilities, with the person forms showing different degrees of grammaticalization following the pronoun–clitic–suffix sequence. This is also substantiated by the very fact that the three person forms are recognized by traditional grammarians of Egyptian as various types of "pronoun."

The grammaticalization of the system of person in general verifies the fact that the realizations of this system turn up at different spots along the lexis-grammar continuum in various languages, and they perform their duties in the overall construal of ideational meaning. Different strategies of meaning construal, including both lexical and grammatical means, are involved in the semogenic process as a unity.

5.4 A brief typological account

The description and exemplification in this book involve multiple languages, and the typological variation in the meaning-making resources of various languages will be tentatively accounted for in this section. The lexicogrammatical system of a certain language can be mapped out as a system of systems distributed in terms

100 *Complementarity between lexis and grammar*

of metafunction and rank; there are some major lexicogrammatical systems that are comparatively stable across languages, but they are subject to considerable typological variation, which tends to increase along with the movement toward more delicate parts of these systems (Matthiessen, 2004: 538–539). The system of person is such a major system manifest across different languages with considerable typological variations.

5.4.1 Ideational metafunction

In terms of the ideational metafunction, an explicit Participant is an essential part in the system of transitivity in many languages such as English and Chinese, and it stands as an independent constituent of a major clause. In contrast to this, the Participant in many Romance languages is usually conflated with the process, with clitics sometimes being a halfway token along the process of grammaticalization. Furthermore, zero person forms leave the clause short of a Participant form altogether, and this piece of meaning is not reflected in the morphology of process but needs to be retrieved from the context of the situation. Zero person forms occur regularly in Japanese clauses where contrived implicitness and uncertainty are often required. The following examples show a comparison of the transitivity structures among three languages.

Example 5.4 Typological difference in transitivity configuration

(a) English:

He	lost	his luggage	at the airport.
Participant: Actor	Process: Material	Participant: Goal	Circumstance: Location

(b) Spanish:

Abrió	la puerta.
Process: Material (+Participant: Actor)	Participant: Goal
"(He/she) opened the door."	

(c) Japanese:

Toukyou no kata	desu ka.
Participant: Value	Process: Relational
"Are (you) from Tokyo?"	

The most nuclear element in the transitivity structure should be the Process, with participants appearing immediately before or after it. However, typological variation across languages may render the form of participant roles (i.e. person) either explicit or implicit, or conflated with the Process. It should be noted that the configurations of experiential elements are largely motivated by interpersonal and textual factors.

5.4.2 Interpersonal metafunction

The making of interpersonal meaning in terms of person also varies from language to language. The presence and position of participant roles in a clause are motivated interpersonally by the function of a clause as an exchange. In the mood structure, Subject is a key component which "supplies the rest of what it takes to form a proposition" (Halliday, 1994: 76). It is responsible with respect to whether the proposition can be affirmed or denied. It is this element that demonstrates significant variations across languages. Any participant roles in the Residue would be more or less alike in that they have the potential of becoming the Subject but are actually not.

In languages like English, various moods are realized by the presence (or absence) and sequence of the Subject and the Finite element; therefore, the presence (or absence) and position of the person form play an important role in realizing interpersonal meaning. And the mood elements (Subject and Finite) can be picked up at the end of a mood-tagged clause in English, a unique feature among languages.

Like English and German, French requires the explicit presence of the Subject in the negotiation of interpersonal meaning in declarative and interrogative clauses. The sequence of the Subject and the Finite element also determines the moods in French; however, this is not the core realization of the French MOOD system. As Caffarel (2004) points out, the grouping of Subject, Finite and Predicator is taken as the Negotiator of the clause, performing various interpersonal functions.

In Romance languages other than French, such as Spanish, Italian and Portuguese, the mood can be negotiated by Finite/Predicator alone, without Subject in unmarked cases.

In Japanese, Subject is not obligatory, too, and so the interpersonal meaning is necessarily enacted by Finite/Predicator and a Negotiator which may indicate both mood and participant identity (see Teruya, 2004).

In languages without any Finite element such as Chinese, the mood, modality and assessment are realized by the Predicator, Adjunct or clausal particles. Since there is no system of finiteness in Chinese, the Subject, as an element semantically bonded with the Predicator to form an arguable proposition, may be "ellipsed." It needs to be presumed from elsewhere, such as from wording or referential meaning (Halliday & McDonald, 2004: 332).

Also in close relation to the system of person within the interpersonal metafunction, the MOOD system in some languages like English or French does not embody a tenor relationship contrast with regard to social status or power relation, while some languages such as Japanese and Korean incorporate politeness and honorification into the system of MOOD so that the participant roles are socially or stylistically enacted.

5.4.3 Textual metafunction

When it comes to textual meaning, there is considerable typological difference among languages in the manifestation of the thematic prominence of person. In languages where Subject typically appears in the initial position, i.e. SVO or SOV languages, the participant as Subject is often given textual prominence positionally. Other participants, if there are any, can realize their textual meaning as Given or New information in the Rheme, or as a marked topical theme in the thematic position, or can acquire textual prominence through intonation.

Languages like Japanese and Korean, though SOV, have their own ways of giving textual prominence rather than simply placing a participant in a textually prominent position, though there is admittedly a position tendency for the topical theme. Such languages bring a particular participant into the spotlight from among the other elements of a clause segmentally by using some postpositional topical markers, e.g. *wa/mo* in Japanese, *neun/eun* in Korean. The segmental realization of textual prominence works in Tagalog, too, except that the topical marker *ang* is prepositional rather than postpositional (see Martin, 1996).

In Romance languages (French excluded) where the Subject is not obligatory, the Process is rendered as the topical Theme, with the conflated pronominal morphology serving as a tracker of discourse participant roles.

In all, strategies for the realization of ideational, interpersonal and textual meaning map onto one another and are mutually supportive and motivating. Typologically, languages tend to be "more congruent in terms of systemic organization than in terms of structural organization" (Matthiessen, 2004: 656). That is, the system of person is a prevalent semantic feature in human language, whereas the actual lexicogrammatical realizations may differ from language to language. The higher the delicacy, the more typological variations are expected to emerge.

5.5 Chapter summary

This chapter started with an elaboration on the term "complementarity" and on the three types of complementarities in language proposed by Halliday, i.e. complementarities between lexis and grammar, between language as system and language as text and between spoken and written language. As a long-standing convention of SFL, the idea of complementarity not only is adopted in its view of natural language but is also reflected in its metalanguage – the set of terms used for the analysis and description of language functioning, such as in metafunctions, axis, agnation, perspective, semogenesis, etc.

Of all three types of complementarity in language, this book focuses on that between lexis and grammar. In construing meaning as either particularity or generality, lexis and grammar play their respective roles along a continuum with different degrees of delicacy. Some phenomena can be looked at either way, since the boundary between the two aspects is obscure. Typologically, the same experience may be construed through varied levels of lexicalization and grammaticalization across languages, which has been verified in terms of the system of person throughout the study. A meaning is also subject to migration along the lexis-grammar continuum diachronically toward either end, which is by no means a transfer across ranks.

With the complexities of the person system and the manifestation of lexical and grammatical realizations of this system previously accounted for, this chapter addresses how the two types of realization complement each other in the construal of meaning related to person. It is suggested that lexis and grammar constitute a balanced entirety for the system of person in the aspects of participant information accessibility, metafunctions and grammaticalization.

Finally, this chapter brings forward a brief typological account from the SFL perspective, i.e. in terms of metafunctions, to examine the typological variation in the genesis of person-related meaning, thus raising the issue of how various languages differ from each other with regard to their idiosyncratic meaning-construing motifs and resources. Different languages may exhibit different formal features in the expression of person; however, they complement each other overall and jointly exercise their function of transforming the meaning about person into specific wording.

Notes

1 The author is indebted to Professor Yan Shiqing, who kindly sent his paper that he had presented at the 12th National Discourse Analysis Conference.
2 It is somewhat atypical in Egyptian usage to adopt an independent pronoun when the predicate is adverbial; however, this possibility is theoretically and technically viable.
3 The equal sign (=) is used by Egyptian grammar convention to indicate suffixation.

6 Conclusion

6.1 Major findings and contributions

This book has provided a comprehensive account of one of the most fundamental and important systems in human language – person. The study is grounded on the theoretical basis of Systemic Functional Linguistics (SFL) and adopts a typological approach, drawing data from a wide variety of languages to investigate features related to person meaning that are either universal or idiosyncratic.

The study sets out to define the range of "person" under discussion. The term "person" in linguistics is commonly taken as synonymous with "personal pronoun," which is but one form of realization of deictic reference to a participant in a speech event. Strictly speaking, "person" in this sense falls into the category of "grammatical person" and on no account represents the actual functioning of language in identifying and distinguishing participant roles in discourses.

Human language offers many resources to enable language users to identify and refer to participants in discourse apart from personal pronouns. Therefore, this book expands the scope of person to any meaning that is loaded with information about participants in discourse and any linguistic expression that manifests such meaning.

Meaning, from the SFL perspective, is made through a series of choices furnished by language as a reservoir of potentials, or probabilities. There have been previous studies on person in the SFL literature centering on either personal pronouns or person as Subject in the mood structure; however, the bigger chunk of the iceberg below the water's surface has to a great extent escaped notice and remained unexplored. In view of this, the third chapter of this book is committed to presenting person as an intricate system, which necessarily involves a string of other systems, i.e. meaning potentials in other categories. These include NOMINALITY, DISCOURSE ROLE, NUMBER, INCLUSIVENESS, GENDER, CASE, REFLEXIVITY, EMPHASIS, HONORIFICATION, PROXIMITY, TOPICALITY, etc.

As a result of systemic studies of person, wide-ranging system networks are devised to characterize the complex nature of the person system. The synthesized (but absolutely not exhaustive) system network of person provided in Figure 3.19 shows how complicated this system can be and what options have to be taken before a concrete person form is finalized. This is the first contribution this study is expected to make.

Resources for expressing meanings are on the stratum of lexicogrammar, with lexis being particularities and grammar generalities. The semantic system of person, when transformed into wording, is realized through either means. Chapter Four is dedicated to the lexicalization and grammaticalization of forms of person. "Lexicalized person forms" refers to those lexical items that make the participant information available, the most straightforward category being nominals. Nominals are employed most commonly to identify non-interacting third person roles in discourse; under special circumstances, they are also used to denote the first and second person, typically with a hint of interpersonal, sociolinguistic and stylistic markedness.

Besides nominals used for denoting entities, person information can also be recognized on processes and qualities, i.e. verbs, adjectives and adverbs. Some of the realizations may not be cross-linguistically universal but may be found only in certain languages. The diverse, or even exotic, means that human languages have to offer confirm that the same domain of meaning can be construed through different language-specific resources.

This principle also holds for the grammaticalization of person. The primary grammatical person form would be personal pronouns, which are generally viewed as a morpho-syntactic class substituting for nouns. There are some prominent pronominal features, as indicated in Section 4.3; however, personal pronouns do not display the same features in all languages, or identical degrees of such features. This study has carried out a comparison among Chinese, English and Japanese personal pronouns with regard to the pronominal features, and located them at different positions along the nominality-pronominality scale first put forward by Sugamoto (1989).

Further grammaticalized person forms after personal pronouns are clitics, inflectional affixes and, ultimately, zero forms. They exhibit different degrees of phonological reduction, morphological dependence, semantic generalization and reliance on the immediate context. The illustration of the full range of lexicalization and grammaticalization of the system of person is this study's second major contribution.

Lexis and grammar, both resources for realizing meaning, are complementary to each other and are the same phenomenon seen from opposite perspectives. The unified lexicogrammar in language users' daily discourse allows them to construe their world experience in more than one way. The fifth chapter of this book brings the focus of this complementary construal of experience to person-related meaning, addressing how lexis and grammar complement each other in the meaning of person and how such meaning is ready to move along the lexis-grammar continuum. It is suggested that the choice of a proper person form is motivated by the participant accessibility in discourse, metafunctions the person form is to fulfill, and the typological features relevant to the specific language.

Language is never a static system, and the same experience is not necessarily construed in the same way among various languages, or at various stages of a single language. Therefore, meaning is apt to migrate across lexical and grammatical regions. The meaning of person is no exception. It appears at varied spots

106 *Conclusion*

with sundry lexical and grammatical forms from both synchronic and diachronic perspectives. The interpretation of lexis-grammar complementarity in terms of the system of person is the third contribution of this study.

6.2 Typological implications

To present the diversity of person-construing methods in human language, as well as a certain commonality among them, this study has adopted a typological approach, observing phenomena and citing examples from a variety of natural languages. The most fundamental characteristic of typology in linguistic analysis has to do with cross-linguistic comparison (Croft, 2003: 1, 6); therefore, some results and implications obtained from cross-linguistic comparison in terms of lexicalization and grammaticalization of person are to be summarized in this section. The summary will focus on a few widely used, major languages which show distinctive and yet representative features in the realization of person meaning.

6.2.1 Chinese

Starting from the lexis end, nominal groups are widely used to refer to third person participants in discourse as in all other languages. Besides, the Chinese language, especially in formal contexts and traditional literature, adopts a broad range of nominal groups to denote the first and second person, mostly with humbleness toward oneself and respect for others. On the grammar side, personal pronouns in Chinese display mixed features of nominality and pronominality, more nominal-like than English but more pronominal than Japanese (see Section 4.3). Neither a person clitic nor a morphological affix has a place in Chinese, but zero forms play a part in tracing participant roles in discourse. The Subject in the mood structure may be either present or presumed, and there is relatively no difference between declarative and imperative structures in the frequency of presence of a personal pronoun Subject (Halliday & McDonald, 2004: 330). The sheer lack of third person nominative pronoun in Old Chinese even necessitates a zero form as an option for the Subject.

6.2.2 English

Nominal groups used in English for referring back to oneself and addressing the second person are not so prolific compared to Chinese, especially the non-vocative usage that falls within the mood structure. Personal pronouns in English exhibit more pronominal characteristics in that they are more limited in number, more inconstant in morphological forms and more restricted in taking modifiers. English has no person clitics except for a few reduced phonological forms of independent accusative pronouns in connected or informal speech. An inflectional suffix indicating person is seen only on the present tense third person singular *-s*, which is deemed a vestige of its Germanic ancestor. Zero forms are regularly found in imperative clauses, clauses with ellipsis, non-finite clauses and casual utterances.

6.2.3 Japanese

One type of lexical indication of person roles that is characteristic of Japanese is achieved by verbs of giving and receiving and verbs of respect and humbleness. Giving and receiving verbs incorporate beneficiary information and directionality of action; social factors and interpersonal relations are lexicalized in honorific and humble verbs. Another characteristic of Japanese is the avoidance of personal pronouns in polite conversation, where nominal expressions are preferred in addressing others. Though generally avoided, Japanese personal pronouns boast more varieties than Chinese and English, thus resembling nominals. Other nominal features of Japanese personal pronouns include the relative consistency in morphology, the sociolinguistic variability and the strong ability to take modifiers. In addition, zero forms are very common in Japanese when the participant roles are evident in the context.

6.2.4 Spanish

Lexically, what is special about Spanish is that the language possesses adverbs denoting participant roles in discourse, namely *conmigo*, *contigo* and *consigo*. The lexicalization of person information in Circumstance is not commonly found in other languages. Grammatically, verb conjugation in Spanish serves the purpose of identifying and referring to person, so that explicit use of independent personal pronouns is ruled out as redundant. When an independent personal pronoun is present in a clause, it realizes a certain textual prominence or interpersonal markedness, not affecting the ideational meaning. The Spanish language also features the use of person clitics, elements at the intermediate stage between independent pronouns and morphological suffixes.

The above four major languages display some typological features related to the construal of person meaning respectively. Other languages may share one or more of the features in a language or combine several features from more than one language. Cross-linguistic comparison and generalization of person-expressing strategies reveal how the participants in speech events are viewed and transformed into meaning against different cultural, social and linguistic backgrounds.

6.3 Limitations and recommendations for further work

As has been discussed in Section 5.1.3, SFL advocates a complementary approach between typology and topology in linguistic analysis. This book pivots around typological studies of the system of person, with little mention of topological issues owing to restrictions of space and study objectives.

The topological approach to the study of the person system is indeed meaningful in that the meaning of person cannot always be represented in a plainly clear-cut way. It is helpful in determining the degree of propinquity of a linguistic phenomenon to features of certain categories and the relative positions of different languages in relation to linguistic features.

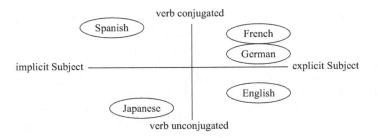

Figure 6.1 Topological representation of person-related features

For example, French and German, though a Romance language and a Germanic language respectively, share some similarities in person forms since they both conjugate their verbs and at the same time require an explicit Subject in declarative clauses. To judge the degree of proximity to features of "explicit Subject" and "verb conjugation," and to compare them with other languages, say English, Japanese and Spanish, in terms of such features, a two-dimensional diagram can be accordingly devised, as in Figure 6.1.

Some linguistic features are more accurately represented in the above diagram. For instance, typologically, Spanish, French and German all have verb conjugation, but, topologically, they have different degrees of conjugation, because the verb conjugation paradigm in Spanish can distinguish all six person features (first, second and third person in singular and plural), whereas French sometimes cannot, and German is still less capable. English still retains a relic *-s*; therefore, it is a little above Japanese, which has no conjugation at all.

If necessary, a third dimension can be readily added, too. The topological perspective facilitates the positioning of several languages in light of any relevant feature, so as to relate them as similar or dissimilar, and to tell in what way they are similar or dissimilar.

In addition to language topology, further studies can also be carried out on the relationships between person forms and other subjects of study in SFL, such as tenor, genre, appraisal, etc. Tenor has to do with the nature of participants, their statuses and roles (Martin & Rose, 2008: 11), and thus it naturally bears a close relationship with the realization of person forms. Specific person forms might have a strong correlation with certain genres or text types, further tied up with particular contexts of culture. For instance, nominal and non-elided person forms are felt to be much preferred in legal documents compared with other genres, say buying and selling service encounters. Moreover, appraisal can also be embodied in choices of person forms, especially in languages where evaluative meaning is heavily loaded in person markers, such as Japanese. The above-mentioned points all deserve serious and in-depth studies and research.

6.4 Coda

Person, the seemingly trivial linguistic system, is ubiquitous in human languages, in their construal of an important experiential aspect of the world and in the negotiation of interpersonal relationships. The study of it does not terminate here, of course, but should go on. SFL views language as a social semiotic, expressing social structure and simultaneously motivated by it. It is eminently reasonable to bring the study of person into such a linguistic framework and continue the exploration.

Lexicalization and grammaticalization are two complementary processes which position meaning at various degrees of delicacy. The current system of person, no matter whether in one single language or in human language as a whole, is at a certain stage of evolution, with bits and pieces spread around different places along the lexis-grammar cline. It is the complementarity between lexis and grammar that comes in to provide the semogenic power and the elasticity for language, including the person system, to adjust itself to the ever-changing eco-social environment.

Bibliography

Akmajian, A. & S. Anderson. 1970. On the use of fourth person in Navajo, or Navajo made harder [J]. *International Journal of American Linguistics*, 36, 1–8.
Andrzejewski, B. W. 1960. The categories of number in noun forms in the Borana dialect of Galla [J]. *Africa*, 30, 62–75.
Ariel, M. 2000. The development of person agreement markers: From pronouns to higher accessibility markers [A]. In: M. Barlow & S. Kemmer (eds.) *Usage-Based Models of Language* [C]. Stanford: CSIL Publications, 197–260.
Bakken, K. 2006. Lexicalization. In: K. Brown (ed.). *Encyclopedia of Language and Linguistics* (2nd ed.) Vol. 7 [M]. Oxford: Elsevier, 106–108.
Bateman, J. A. 1989. Dynamic systemic-functional grammar: A new frontier [J]. *Word*, 40(1–2), 263–286.
Bennett, C. E. 1908. *A Latin Grammar* [M]. Norwood, MA: Norwood Press.
Benson, J., M. J. Cummings & W. S. Greaves. (eds.) 1988. *Linguistics in a Systemic Perspective* [C]. Amsterdam: Benjamins.
Benson, J. & W. S. Greaves. (eds.) 1985. *Systemic Perspectives on Discourse, Vol. 1 & 2: Selected Theoretical Papers from the Ninth International Systemic Workshop* [C]. Norwood: Ablex.
Benveniste, E. 1971. *Problems in General Linguistics* [M]. Translated by Mary Elizabeth Meek. Cora Gables, FA: University of Miami Papers.
Berry, M. 1975. *Introduction to Systemic Linguistics: 1, Structures and Systems* [M]. London: Batsford.
Berry, M. 1977. *Introduction to Systemic Linguistics: 2, Levels and Links* [M]. London: Batsford.
Berry, M. 1982. Review of Halliday 1978 [J]. *Nottingham Linguistic Circular*, 11, 64–94.
Biermann, A. 1982. Die grammatische Kategorie Numerus [A]. In: H. Seiler & C. Lehmann (eds.) *Apprehension: Das sprachliche Erfassen von Gegenständen I: Bereich und Ordnung der Phänomene* [C]. Tübingen: Narr, 229–243.
Blake, B. J. 2001. *Case* (2nd ed.) [M]. Cambridge: Cambridge University Press.
Bloomfield, L. 1933. *Language* [M]. New York: Henry Holt.
Boas, F. 1911. *Handbook of American Indian Languages* [M]. Washington: Government Printing Office.
Booij, G. E. et al. (eds.) 2004. Booij, G. E., C. Lehmann, J. Mudgan & S. Skopeteas (eds.) *Morphology: An International Handbook on Inflection and Word-Formation* [M]. Berlin: de Gruyter Mouton.
Bosch, P. 1983. *Agreement and Anaphora* [M]. London: Academic Press.
Bosque, I. & V. Demonte. 1999. *Grammática Descriptiva de la Lengua Española* [M]. Madrid: Espasa.
Braun, F. 1988. *Terms of Address: Problems of Patterns and Usage in Various Languages and Cultures* [M]. Berlin/New York/Amsterdam: Mouton de Gruyter.

Bright, W. (ed.) 1992. *International Encyclopedia of Linguistics* [M]. Oxford: Oxford University Press.
Brinton, L. J. & E. C. Traugott. 2005. *Lexicalization and Language Change* [M]. Cambridge: Cambridge University Press.
Brown, K. (ed.) 2006. *Encyclopedia of Language and Linguistics* (2nd ed.) [M]. Oxford: Elsevier.
Brown, P. & S. C. Levinson. 1987. *Politeness* [M]. Cambridge: Cambridge University Press.
Butler, C. S. 1985. *Systemic Linguistics: Theory and Applications* [M]. London: Batsford Academic and Educational.
Caffarel, A. 2004. Metafunctional profile of the grammar of French [A]. In: A. Caffareal, J. R. Martin & C. M. I. M. Matthiessen (eds.) *Language Typology: A Functional Perspective* [C]. Amsterdam/Philadelphia: John Benjamins, 77–138.
Caffarel, A., J. R. Martin & C. M. I. M. Matthiessen. (eds.) 2004. *Language Typology: A Functional Perspective* [C]. Amsterdam/Philadelphia: John Benjamins.
Carter, R. & D. Burton (eds.) 1982. *Literary Text and Language Study* [C]. London: Edward Arnold.
Chomsky, N. 1965. *Aspects of the Theory of Syntax* [M]. Cambridge, MA: MIT Press.
Chomsky, N. 1981. *Lectures on Government and Binding* [M]. Dordrecht: Foris.
Clark, E. V. 1993. *The Lexicon in Acquisition* [M]. Cambridge: Cambridge University Press.
Comrie, B. 1981. *Language Universals and Linguistic Typology* [M]. Oxford: Blackwell.
Corbett, G. G. 1991. *Gender* [M]. Cambridge: Cambridge University Press.
Corbett, G. G. 2000. *Number* [M]. Cambridge: Cambridge University Press.
Corbett, G. G. 2006. Gender, grammatical. In: K. Brown (ed.). *Encyclopedia of Language and Linguistics* (2nd ed.) Vol. 4 [M]. Oxford: Elsevier, 749–756.
Cornish, F. 1999. *Anaphora, Discourse and Understanding* [M]. Oxford: Oxford University Press.
Croft, W. 2003. *Typology and Universals* (2nd ed.) [M]. Cambridge: Cambridge University Press.
Crystal, D. 1985. *A Dictionary of Linguistics and Phonetics* (2nd ed.) [M]. New York: Basil Blackwell.
Cysouw, M. 2003. *The Paradigmatic Structure of Person Marking* [M]. Oxford: Oxford University Press.
Delisle, G. L. 1973. On the so-called fourth person in Algonquian [J]. *Working Papers on Language Universals*, 12, 69–83.
Deng, R. H. 2009. A systemic representation of the verbs in the existential enhanced theme construction [A]. In: Huang Guowen (ed.) *Studies in Functional Linguistics and Discourse Analysis (I)* [C]. Beijing: Higher Education Press, 74–88.
Dixon, R. M. W. 1979. Ergativity [J]. *Language*, 55(1), 59–138.
Dixon, R. M. W. 1980. *The Languages of Australia* [M]. Cambridge: Cambridge University Press.
Eggins, S. 2004. *An Introduction to Systemic Functional Linguistics* (2nd ed.) [M]. New York/London: Continuum.
Fawcett, R. P. In press for 2017 a. *The Functional Syntax Handbook: Analyzing English at the Level of Form* [M]. London: Equinox.
Fawcett, R. P. forthcoming b. *The Functional Semantics Handbook: Analyzing English at the Level of Meaning* [M]. London: Equinox.
Fawcett, R. P. 1975. Summary of "some issues concerning levels in systemic models of language" [J]. *Nottingham Linguistic Circular*, 4, 24–37.
Fawcett, R. P. 1980. *Cognitive Linguistics and Social Interaction: Towards an Integrated Model of s Systemic Functional Grammar and the Other Components of a Communicating Mind* [M]. Heidelberg: Julius Groos.

Fawcett, R. P. 1987. The semantics of clause and verb for relational processes in English [A]. In: M. A. K. Halliday & R. P. Fawcett (eds.) *New Developments in Systemic Linguistics, Vol. 1: Theory and Description* [C]. London: Pinter, 130–183.

Fawcett, R. P. 1988. The English personal pronouns: An exercise in linguistic theory [A]. In: James D. Benson, Michael J. Cummings & William S. Greaves (eds.) *Linguistics in a Systemic Perspective* [C]. Amsterdam/Philadelphia: John Benjamins, 185–220.

Fawcett, R. P. 2008. *Invitation to Systemic Functional Linguistics through the Cardiff Grammar: An Extension and Simplification of Halliday's Systemic Functional Grammar* (3rd ed.) [M]. London: Equinox.

Fawcett, R. P. 2009. A semantic system network for MOOD in English [A]. In: Zhang Jingyuan, Peng Yi & He Wei (eds.) *Current Issues in Systemic Functional Linguistics—Papers from the 8th Chinese Systemics Week* [C]. Beijing: Foreign Language Teaching and Research Press, 3–62.

Firth, J. R. 1948. The semantics of linguistic science [J]. *Lingua*, 1, 393–404. Reprinted in Firth 1957, 139–147.

Firth, J. R. 1950. Personality and language in society [J]. *Sociological Review*, 42, 37–52. Reprinted in Firth 1957, 177–189.

Firth, J. R. 1951. General linguistics and descriptive grammar [J]. *Transaction of the Philological Society*, 50(1), 69–87. Reprinted in Firth 1957, 216–230.

Firth, J. R. 1957. *Papers in Linguistics 1934–1951* [M]. London: Oxford University Press.

Fleck, D. W. 2008. Coreferential fourth-person pronouns in Matses [J]. *International Journal of American Linguistics*, 74(3), 279–311.

Forchheimer, P. 1953. *The Category of Person in Language* [M]. Berlin: Walter de Gruyter.

Gardiner, A. H. 1957. *Egyptian Grammar* (3rd ed.) [M]. London: Oxford University Press.

Givón, T. 1976. Topic, pronoun, and grammatical agreement [A]. In: C. N. Li (ed.) *Subject and Topic* [C]. New York: Academic Press, 149–188.

Givón, T. 1979. *On Understanding Grammar* [M]. New York: Academic Press.

Gouveia, C. A. M. 2007. Address forms and the interpersonal organization of the Portuguese clause. Presentation at the 34th International Systemic Functional Congress, Odense, Denmark.

Grasserie, R. de la. 1888. *Etudes de Grammaire Comparée: De la véritable nature du pronom* [M]. Louvain: Imprimerie Lefever frères et soeur.

Greenberg, J. H. 1966. *Language Universals, with Special Reference to Feature Hierarchies* [M]. The Hague: Mouton.

Halliday, M. A. K. 1956. Grammatical categories in modern Chinese [J]. *Transactions of the Philological Society, 55)1)*, 177–224.

Halliday, M. A. K. 1961. Categories of the theory of grammar [J]. *Word*, 17(3), 241–292.

Halliday, M. A. K. 1966. Some notes on "deep" grammar [J]. *Journal of Linguistics*, 2(1), 57–67.

Halliday, M. A. K. 1969. Options and functions in the English clause [J]. *Brno Studies in English*, 8, 81–88.

Halliday, M. A. K. 1975. *Learning How to Mean* [M]. London: Edward Arnold.

Halliday, M. A. K. 1978. *Language as Social Semiotic: The Social Interpretation of Language and Meaning* [M]. London: Arnold.

Halliday, M. A. K. 1985a/1994. *An Introduction to Functional Grammar* [M]. London: Edward Arnold.

Halliday, M. A. K. 1985b. Systemic background [A]. In: James D. Benson & William S. Greaves (eds.) *Systemic Perspectives on Discourse* [C]. New York: Ablex publishing, 1–15.

Halliday, M. A. K. 1987. Spoken and written modes of meaning [A]. In: Rosalind Horowitz & S. Jay Samuels (eds.) *Comprehending Oral and Written Language* [C]. New York: Academic Press, 55–82.

Halliday, M. A. K. 1992a. How do you mean? [A]. In: Martin Davies & Louise Ravelli (eds.) *Advances in Systemic Linguistics: Recent Theory and Practice* [C]. New York: Pinter, 20–35.
Halliday, M. A. K. 1992b. The act of meaning [A]. In: James E. Alatis (ed.) *Georgetown University Round Table on Languages and Linguistics: Language, Communication and Social Meaning* [C]. Washington: Georgetown University Press, 7–21.
Halliday, M. A. K. 1995. Computing meaning: Some reflections on past experience and present prospects [A]. Paper presented to PACLING 95, Brisbane.
Halliday, M. A. K. 1996. On grammar and grammatics [A]. In: R. Hasan, C. Cloran & D. G. Butt (eds.) *Functional Descriptions: Theory in Practice* [C]. Amsterdam: John Benjamins, 1–38.
Halliday, M. A. K. 1997. Linguistics as metaphor [A]. In: Anne-Marie Simon-Vandenbergen, Kristin Davidse & Dirk Noel (eds.) *Reconnecting Language: Morphology and Syntax in Functional Perspectives* [C]. Amsterdam: Benjamins, 3–27.
Halliday, M. A. K. 2008. *Complementarities in Language* [M]. Beijing: Commercial Press.
Halliday, M. A. K. & W. S. Greaves. 2008. *Intonation in the Grammar of English* [M]. London/Oakville: Equinox.
Halliday, M. A. K. & R. Hasan. 1976. *Cohesion in English* [M]. London: Longman.
Halliday, M. A. K. & E. McDonald. 2004. Metafunctional profile of the grammar of Chinese [A]. In: A. Caffarel, J. R. Martin & C. M. I. M. Matthiessen (eds.) *Language Typology: A Functional Perspective* [C]. Amsterdam/Philadelphia: John Benjamins, 305–396.
Halliday, M. A. K. & C. M. I. M. Matthiessen. 1999. *Construing Experience through Meaning: A Language-Based Approach to Cognition* [M]. London/New York: Continuum.
Halliday, M. A. K. & C. M. I. M. Matthiessen. 2004. *An Introduction to Functional Grammar* (3rd ed.) [M]. London: Hodder Arnold.
Harley, H. & E. Ritter. 2002. Person and number in pronouns: A feature-geometric analysis [J]. *Language*, 78(3), 482–526.
Hasan, R. 1987. The grammarian's dream: Lexis as most delicate grammar [A]. In: M. A. K. Halliday & R. Fawcett (eds.) *New Developments in Systemic Linguistics, Vol. 1: Theory and Description* [C]. London: Pinter, 184–211.
Hayward, R. J. 1979. Bayso revisited: Some preliminary linguistic observations II [J]. *Bulletin of the School of Oriental and African Studies, University of London*, 42, 101–132.
Head, B. F. 1978. Respect degrees in pronominal reference [A]. In: J. H. Greenberg, C. A. Ferguson & E. A. Moravcsik (eds.) *Universals of Human Language, Vol. 3* [C]. Stanford: Stanford University Press, 151–211.
Hjelmslev, L. 1953. *Prolegomena to a Theory of Language* [M]. Translated by F. J. Whitefeld. Baltimore: Waverly Press.
Hockett, C. F. 1958. *A Course in Modern Linguistics* [M]. New York: Macmillan.
Hoey, M. (ed.) 1993. *Data, Description and Discourse: Papers on the English Language in Honour of John McH: Sinclair* [C]. London: HarperCollins.
Hopper, P. J. 1992. Grammaticalization. In: W. Bright (ed.) *International Encyclopedia of Linguistics* [M]. Oxford: Oxford University Press, 79–81.
Hopper, P. J. & E. C. Traugott. 2003. *Grammaticalization* [M]. Cambridge: Cambridge University Press.
Hu, Z. L. 2006. *Linguistics: A Course Book* (3rd ed.) [M]. Beijing: Peking University Press.
Huang, Y. 2007. The grammaticalization and lexicalization of space deixis: A cross-linguistic analysis [J]. *Journal of Foreign Languages*, 30(1), 2–18.
Hudson, R. A. 1967. Constituency in a systemic description of the English clause [J]. *Lingua*, 18, 225–250.
Hudson, R. A. 1971. *English Complex Sentences: An Introduction to Systemic Grammar* [M]. Amsterdam/London: North Holland Publishing.

Hudson, R. A. 1974. Systemic generative grammar [J]. *Linguistics*, 139, 5–42.
Hudson, R. A. 1978. Daughter-dependency grammar and systemic grammar [J]. *UEA Papers in Linguistics*, 6, 1–14.
Hudson, R. A. 1982. Word grammar [A]. Preprints of the Plenary Session Papers, XIIIth International Congress of Linguistics, Tokyo 1982 [C], 77–86.
Hudson, R. A. 2007. *Language Networks: The New Word Grammar* [M]. Oxford/New York: Oxford University Press.
Irwin, B. 1974. *Salt Yui Grammar* [M]. Canberra: Dept. of Linguistics, Australian National University.
Jackendoff, R. 2007. *Language, Consciousness, Culture: Essays on Mental Structure* [M]. Cambridge, MA: The MIT Press.
Jacobsen, W. H. 1979. Noun and verb in Nootkan [A]. In: B. S. Efrat (ed.) *The Victorian Conference on Northwestern Languages* [C]. Victoria, BC: British Columbia Provincial Museum, 83–155.
Jakobson, R. 1971. Shifters, verbal categories, and the Russian verb [A]. In: R. Jakobson (ed.) *Selected Writings, Vol. 2* [C]. The Hague: Mouton, 130–147.
Jespersen, O. 1924. *The Philosophy of Grammar* [M]. London: Allen and Unwin.
Kattán-Ibarra, J. & C. J. Pountain. 2003. *Modern Spanish Grammar: A Practical Guide* (2nd ed.) [M]. London/New York: Routledge.
Koehn, E. & S. Koehn. 1986. Apalai [A]. In: D. C. Derbyshire & G. K. Pullum (eds.) *Handbook of Amazonian Languages, Vol. 1* [C]. Berlin: Mouton de Gruyter, 33–127.
Lakoff, G. 1987. *Women, Fire and Dangerous Things: What Categories Reveal about the Mind* [M]. Chicago: University of Chicago Press.
Langacker, R. W. 1987. *Foundations of Cognitive Grammar, Vol. 1: Theoretical Prerequisites* [M]. Stanford, CA: Stanford University Press.
Lange, R. A. 1988. *501 Japanese Verbs* [M]. New York: Barron's Educational Series, Inc.
Lee, I. & S. R. Ramsey. 2000. *The Korean Language* [M]. Albany: State University of New York Press.
Lehmann, C. 1987. On the function of agreement [A]. In: M. Barlow & C. A. Ferguson (eds.) *Agreement in Natural Language* [C]. Stanford: CSLI, 55–65.
Lemke, J. L. 1999. Typological and topological meaning in diagnostic discourse [J]. *Discourse Processes*, 27(2), 173–185.
Love, J. R. B. 2000. *The Grammatical Structure of the Worora Language of North-Western Australia* [M]. Munich: Lincom Europa.
Lyons, J. 1977. *Semantics* [M]. Cambridge: Cambridge University Press.
Marlett, S. A. 1990. Person and number inflection in Seri [J]. *International Journal of American Linguistics*, 56(4), 503–541.
Martin, J. R. 1983. Participant identification in English, Tagalog and Kate [J]. *Australian Journal of Linguistics*, 3(1), 45–74.
Martin, J. R. 1985. Process and text: Two aspects of human semiosis [A]. In: J. D. Benson & W. S. Greaves (eds.) *Systemic Perspectives on Discourse Vol. 1: Selected Theoretical Papers from the 9th International Systemic Workshop* [C]. Norwood, NJ: Ablex Publishing Corporation, 248–274.
Martin, J. R. 1992. *English Text: System and Structure* [M]. Philadelphia/Amsterdam: John Benjamins.
Martin, J. R. 1996. Transitivity in Tagalog: A functional interpretation of case [A]. In: M. Berry, C. Butler, R. Fawcett & G. Huang (eds.) *Meaning and Form: Systemic Functional Interpretations* [C]. New Jersey: Ablex Publishing Corporation, 229–296.
Martin, J. R. & C. M. I. M. Matthiessen. 1991. Systemic typology and topology [A]. In: F. Christie (ed.) *Literacy in Social Processes* [C]. Darwin: Centre for Studies of Language in Education, Northern Territory University, 345–383.
Martin, J. R., C. M. I. M. Matthiessen & C. Painter. 1997. *Working with Functional Grammar* [M]. London: Arnold.

Martin, J. R., C. M. I. M. Matthiessen & C. Painter. 2010. *Deploying Functional Grammar* [M]. Beijing: The Commercial Press.
Martin, J. R. & R. McCormack. 2001. Mapping meaning: Profiling with integrity in a postmodern world [J]. *Applied Language Studies*, 1(1), 6–18.
Martin, J. R. & D. Rose. 2008. *Genre Relations: Mapping Culture* [M]. London/Oakville: Equinox.
Martin, J. R. & P. R. R. White. 2005. *The Language of Evaluation: Appraisal in English* [M]. Basingstoke/New York: Palgrave Macmillan.
Matthiessen, C. M. I. M. 1990. Lexico(grammatical) choice in text generation [A]. In: Cecile Paris, William Swartout & William C. Mann (eds.) *Natural Language Generation in Artificial Intelligence and Computational Linguistics* [C]. Dordrecht: Kluwer, 249–292.
Matthiessen, C. M. I. M. 1995. *Lexicogrammatical Cartography: English Systems* [M]. Tokyo/Taipei/Dallas: International Language Sciences Publishers.
Matthiessen, C. M. I. M. 2004. Descriptive motifs and generalizations [A]. In: A. Caffarel, J. R. Martin & C. M. I. M. Matthiessen. (eds.) *Language Typology: A Functional Perspective* [C]. Amsterdam/Philadelphia: John Benjamins, 537–673.
Matthiessen, C. M. I. M. & J. Bateman. 1991. *Systemic Linguistics and Text Generation: Experiences from Japanese and English* [M]. London: Frances Pinter.
Matthiessen, C. M. I. M. & M. A. K. Halliday. 2009. *Systemic Functional Grammar: A First Step into the Theory* [M]. Beijing: Higher Education Press.
McClure, W. 2000. *Using Japanese: A Guide to Contemporary Usage* [M]. Cambridge: Cambridge University Press.
Meillet, A. 1912. L'évolution des formes grammaticales [J]. *Scientia (Rivista di scienza)* 12(26), 384–400. Reprinted in Meillet 1958. In: *Linguistique Historique et Linguistique Générale* [C]. Paris: Champion, 130–148.
Palmer, F. R. (ed.) 1968. *Selected Papers of J. R. Firth, 1952–1959* [C]. Bloomington & London: Indiana University Press.
Poynton, C. 1990. *Address and the Semiotics of the Social Relations: A Systemic Functional Account of Address Forms and Practices in Australian English* [D]. Sydney: University of Sydney.
Price, G. 1993. *A Comprehensive French Grammar* [M]. Oxford, UK & Cambridge, MA, USA: Blackwell.
Proudfoot, A. & F. Cardo. 1997. *Modern Italian Grammar: A Practical Guide* [M]. London/New York: Routledge.
Quirk, R., S. Greenbaum, G. Leech & J. Svartvik. 1985. *A Comprehensive Grammar of the English Language* [M]. London: Longman.
Ramat, P. 2001. Degrammaticalization or transcategorization? [A]. In: C. Schaner-Wolles, J. Rennison & F. Neubarth (eds.) *Naturally! Linguistic Studies in Honour of Wolfgang Ulrich Dressler Presented on the Occasion of his 60th Birthday* [C]. Torino: Rosenbach and Sellier, 393–401.
Rini, J. 1990. On the chronology of Spanish *conmigo, contigo, consigo* and the interaction of phonological, syntactic, and morphological processes [J]. *Hispanic Review*, 58(4), 503–512.
Sapir, E. 1921. *Language: An Introduction to the Study of Speech* [M]. New York: Harcourt, Brace & World, Inc.
Saussure, F. de. 1916/1960. *Course in General Linguistics* [M]. Translated by W. Baskin. London: Peter Owen.
Scotton, C. M. & W. Zhu. 1983. Tóngzhì in China: Language change and its conversational consequences [J]. *Language in Society*, 12(4), 477–494.
Siewierska, A. 2004. *Person* [M]. Cambridge: Cambridge University Press.
Sinclair, J. 1987. Collocation: A progress report [A]. In: R. Steele & T. Threadgold (eds.) *Language Topics: Essays in Honour of Michael Halliday* [C]. Amsterdam: John Benjamins, 319–312.

Steele, S. 1977. Clisis and diachrony [A]. In: C. N. Li (ed.) *Mechanisms of Syntactic Change* [C]. Austin: University of Texas Press, 539–579.

Stenzler, A. F. 1915. *Elementarbuch der Sanskrit-Sprache: Grammatik, Text, Wörterbuch* [M]. Giessen: Verlag von Alfred Töpelmann.

Stubbs, M. 1996. *Text and Corpus Analysis* [M]. Oxford: Blackwell.

Sugamoto, N. 1989. Pronominality: A noun-pronoun continuum [A]. In: Roberta Corrigan, Fred Eckman and Michael Noonan (eds.) *Linguistic Categorization* [C]. Amsterdam: John Benjamins, 267–291.

Teruya, K. 2004. Metafunctional profile of the grammar of Japanese [A]. In: A. Caffarel, J. R. Martin & C. M. I. M. Matthiessen (eds.) *Language Typology: A Functional Perspective* [C]. Amsterdam/Philadelphia: John Benjamins, 185–254.

Teruya, K. 2006. *A Systemic Functional Grammar of Japanese* [M]. London/New York: Continuum.

Tucker, G. H. 1998. *The Lexicogrammar of Adjectives: A Systemic Functional Approach to Lexis* [M]. London/New York: Cassell.

Tucker, G. H. 2005. Extending the lexicogrammar: Towards a more comprehensive account of extraclausal, partially clausal and non-clausal expressions in spoken discourse [J]. *Language Sciences*, 27(6), 679–709.

Tucker, G. H. 2007. Between lexis and grammar: Towards a systemic functional approach to phraseology [A]. In: R. Hasan, C. M. I. M. Matthiessen & J. J. Webster (eds.) *Continuing Discourse on Language: A Functional Perspective, Vol. 2* [C]. London/Oakville: Equinox, 953–977.

van Ginneken, J. 1907. *Principles de Linguistique Psychologique* [M]. Paris: Rivière.

Ventola, E. 1987. *The Structure of Social Interaction: A Systemic Approach to the Semiotics of Service Encounters* [M]. London: Frances Pinter.

Wischer, I. 2006. Grammaticalization. In: K. Brown (ed.). *Encyclopedia of Language and Linguistics* (2nd ed.) Vol. 5 [M]. Oxford: Elsevier, 129–136.

Wundt, W. 1911. *Probleme der Völkerpsychologie* [M]. Leipzig: Wiegandt.

Zwicky, A. M. 1977. *On Clitics* [M]. Bloomington, IN: Indiana University Linguistics Club.

Zwicky, A. M. 1985. Clitics and particles [J]. *Language*, 61(2), 283–305.

Zwicky, A. M. 1987. Suppressing the Zs [J]. *Journal of Linguistics*, 83(1), 133–148.

Zwicky, A. M. 1994. What is a clitic [A]. In: J. A. Nevis, B. D. Joseph, D. Wanner & A. M. Zwicky (eds.) *Clitics—A Comprehensive Bibliography 1982–1991* [C]. Amsterdam/Philadelphia: John Benjamins, xii-xx.

Zwicky, A. M. & G. K. Pullum. 1983. Cliticization vs. inflection: English n't [J]. *Language*, 59(3), 502–513.

陈榴 (Chen, L.). 2007.《东去的语脉：韩国汉字词语研究》[M]. 大连：辽宁师范大学出版社.

程雨民 (Cheng, Y.). 1993. 汉语中词汇和语法的互补[A]. 朱永生主编：《语言·语篇·语境》[C]. 北京：清华大学出版社, 158–166.

丁椿寿、朱文旭、李生福 (Ding, C., W. Zhu & S. Li). 1991.《现代彝语》[M]. 北京：中央民族学院出版社.

胡壮麟、朱永生、张德禄、李战子 (Hu, Z., Y. Zhu, D. Zhang & Z. Li). 2008.《系统功能语言学概论》（修订版）[M]. 北京：北京大学出版社.

胡壮麟、叶起昌 (Hu, Z. & Q. Ye). 2010.《语言学理论与流派》[M]. 北京：高等教育出版社.

刘丹青、强星娜 (Liu, D. & X. Qiang). 2009.《人称范畴》介评[J].《南开语言学刊》8(1), 156–166.

裴文 (Pei, W.). 2007.《梵语通论》[M]. 北京：人民出版社.

王力 (Wang, L.). 1980.《汉语史稿》[M]. 北京：中华书局.

王鸣 (Wang, M.). 2003. 日本社会与日语第二人称代词[J].《浙江大学学报（人文社会科学版）》33(4), 89–94.

王品 (Wang, P.). 2010. 系统功能语言学的互补思想——M. A. K. Halliday新著 *Complementarities in Language*述介[J]. 《外国语》33(2), 20–25.
严世清 (Yan, S.). 2010. 意义进化的机制及其理据. 第十二届全国语篇分析研讨会报告. 上海：同济大学.
朱永生 (Zhu, Y.). 2005. 《语境动态研究》[M]. 北京：北京大学出版社.
朱永生, 严世清 (Zhu, Y. & S. Yan). 2001. 《系统功能语言学多维思考》[M]. 上海：上海外语教育出版社.

Index

addressee 1, *30*, 33, 37–9, 41, 49, *52*, *55*, 59, 61, 63, 67, 75, 83, 95
addresser 1, 33, *52*, 59, 61–3, 67, 83, 95; *see also* speaker
adjective 2–3, 7, 24, 26, 42, 45, 57, 68–9, 81–3, 94, 105
adverb 7, 24, 26, 57, 69–70, 83, 94, 105, 107
affix 30, 47, 49, 53, 71–6, 80, 83–4, 97–8, 105–6; *see also* suffix
agnation 88–9, 91, 102
animacy 5, 7, 39
appraisal 5, 60, 87, 97, 108
aspect 3, 54, 71, 74
axis 87–8, *91*, 102

beneficiary 67, 107
Berry, M 19–20, 24

Cantonese 43
case 3, 7, 29, 31, 42–4; 47, *55*, 59, 71, *79*, 80, 104; ablative 44; accusative 43, 45, *55*, 77, 80–1, 106; dative 43–4; genitive *43*, 44–5, *55*, 77; locative 44; nominative 1, 31, 40, *43*, *55*, 77, 84, 106
Chinese 4, 6, 35–7, 40, 43–4, 46, 51, 59–63, 65, 68, 76–82, 84–6, 92–4, 95, 98, 100–1, 105–7
circumstance 59, 69, 83, 100, 107
class 4–5, 13, 69–70
clause 4, 7, 15, *18*, 20, 25–6, 29, 31, 42–5, 47, 53, 59, 61, 64, 66–7, 69–70, 74–7, 82, 86, 92, *93*, 95, 98–102, 106–8
cline 23–4, 72; of grammaticality 71; of grammaticalization 76; lexis-grammar 49, 58, 70, 84–5, 92–4, 96, 99, 109; nominality-pronominality 8, 81–2; *see also* continuum
clitic 30, 45–7, 71–6, 83–4, 94, 96–100, 105–7; simple 73; special 73–4

complementarity 85–6, 102; in language 86; in SFL metalanguage 87–92; lexis and grammar 6, 8–9, 26, 28, 84–5, 92–9, 105–6, 109
content plane 14, 22
context 10, 13, 20, 22, 25, 30–1, 33, 53, 62–3, 71, 76, 79, 81, 84, 100, 105–8
continuum 27; lexis-grammar 6, 8, 58, 71, 92, *93*, 94–5, 97–9, 102–3, 105; nominality-pronominality 79, 83

definiteness 3, 54, 56n3
delicacy 4, 8, 15–16, 17, 19–20, 23, 31–2, 38, 95, 102, 109
discourse 2, 6, 20, 26, 30–1, 33, 38–9, 42, 44, 47, 53–4, 61–2, 64, 67–71, 75, 78, 79–80, 82–3, 85, 89, 95–7, 102, 104–6; event 3; role 2, 5, 7, 30–1, 33–4, 38, 40, *41*, 47, 49, *50*, *55*, 57–9, 62, 67–8, 73, 77–8, 83, 96, 104–7

Egyptian 99, 103n2–3
element 4–5, 7, 11–14, 29, 32, 69–70, 87–8, 92, 101
English 4–6, 15–16, 18–19, 25–9, 33, 35–7, 39–40, 44–9, 51–2, 59, 61–3, 65, 68–71, 73, 75–7, 79–82, 84n3, 88, 94, 95, 100–1, 105–8; Modern 15, 43, 75, 83; Old 15
entity 7, 10, 33, 35, 58, 95–6
expression plane 14, 22

Fawcett, R. P. 5, 18–20, 25–6, 28–9, 40
Firth, J. R. 10–13
Functional Linguistics *see* Systemic Functional Linguistics

gender 3, 5, 7, 15, 33, 39–44, 46, 49, 51, *55*, 59, 71, 74, 98, 104; feminine 3, 15,

Index 119

33, 39–41, *43*, 50, *55*; and inclusiveness 41; masculine 3, 15, 33, 39–42, *43*, 53, *55*; neuter 15, 33, 39–41, *43*, *55*; and number and discourse role 40–1
German 3, 15, 35, 39, 43, 50, 94, 101, 106, 108
glossematics 11
grammar 3–14, 16–17, 21–8, 40, 57–8, 70, 74, 84–6, 92–9, 102–3, 105–6, 109; Cardiff 18, 25–6; Functional 10, 26, 32, 70; Scale and Category 4, 13, 23; Systemic 13, 16, 20, 24; *see also* lexicogrammar
grammatical category 3–6, 46, 54
grammaticalization 6–9, 57–8, 70–6, 83, 95, 97–100, 102–3, 105–6, 109

Halliday, M. A. K. 4, 5, 10–11, 13–14, 16, 18–24, 30, 54, 86, 90, 92–3, 102; and Hasan 51; and Matthiessen 5, 29, 69, 92, 94
Hasan, R. 23–5
Hjelmslev, L. 10–11
honorification 3, 49–51, *55*, 67, 78, 80, 98, 101, 104, 107
Hudson, R. A. 16–17

inclusiveness 3, 7, 36–9, 41, *55*, 104
Indo-European languages 39, 74–5, 77, 79, 83
inflection 2, 7, 30, 42, 44, 59, 71–5, 83, 94, 97–9, 105–6
interactant *30*, 33, *34*, *38*, 49, *55*, 78, 90
intimacy 5, 61, 80, 83
Italian 44, 45, 47, 49–50, 75, 83, 101

Jackendoff, R. 27–8
Japanese 19, 35, 44, 49–50, 52–3, 65–7, 77, 79–83, 94, 98, 100–2, 105–8

Korean 44, 50, 52–3, 65–6, 98, 101–2

Langacker, R. W. 26–7
Latin 1, 2, 33, 39, 40, 42–3, 51, 59, 73–4, 79
lexical item 1, 6–8, 23–5, 27–8, 57–8, 68–71, 83–4, 92–4, 97–8, 105
lexicalization 6–9, 57–8, 66–8, 71, 83, 95, 102, 105–7, 109
lexical unit 34, 57
lexicogrammar 5, 6, 8–10, 21–6, 28–9, 31, 49, 58, 70, 85–7, 92–5, 99–100, 102, 105
lexicon 7, 23, 26–8, 57–8, 71, 85

lexis 6–8, 23–6, 28, 57–8, 71, 84–6, 92–3, 95–9, 102–3, 105–6, 109; as most delicate grammar 8, 23–5, 93; *see also* lexical item; lexical unit
logogenesis *see* semogenesis

Malinowski, B. 10
Martin, J. R. 33, 84n5, 89
Matthiessen, C. M. I. M. 19, 25
metafunction 5, 24–5, 30, 53, 87, *88*, *91*, 95–7, 100, 101–3, 105
modality 3, *18*, 70, 87, 94, 97, 101
mood 3, 5, 7, 15, 16, 18, 29, 54, 64, 71, 74–7, 87–8, 94, 97, 101, 104, 106

nominal expression 2, 32, 35–6, 38, 52, 57, 77, 107
nominal group 32, 58–9, 61–5, 68, 79–80, 83, 98, 106
nominality 8, 31–3, 34, *55*, 79–81, *82*, 104–6
noun 3, 7–8, 24–5, 31–2, 34–6, 39–44, 46, 51, 54, 57, 59–63, 66, 68, 78–80, 83, 86, 105
number 3, 5, 7, 15, 31, 34–8, 40, *41*, 43–4, 46–7, 49–52, *55*, 59, 70–1, 74, *79*, 80–2, 98, 104; dual 15, 35–6, *37*, *39*; other 36; plural 1, 3, 15, 35–41, *43*, 45, 49–52, *55*, 68, 74, 80–1, 86, 108; singular 1, 3, 15, 31, 33, 35–9, *40*, *41*, *43*, 45, 47, 49, 51–3, *55*, 59, 74, 75, 80, 84, 98, 106, 108; trial 35; unspecified 36

ontogenesis *see* semogenesis

paradigmatic relation 4, 11–14, 16, 20, 87–8
participant 1, 3, 29–31, 33, 38–9, 44–5, 59, 62, 64, 66, 68, 70, 74–80, 83, 95–6, 100–8; accessibility 31, 95–6, 103, 105; role 3, 6, 25, 30–2, 54, 57–9, 66–8, 70, 74–5, 77–8, 83, 96, 100–2, 104, 106–7
person: category 3, 5–6, 54; dichotomy 2–3; first 1–3, 7, 33, 36–8, 41, 45, 47, 49, 52, 59–63, 66–8, 80–1, 83, 98, 105–6, 108; form 2–3, 5, 7–8, 28, 30–1, 33, 35, 39–41, 43–4, 47–50, 53–4, 62, 64, 71–2, 74, 76–9, 84–5, 95, 97–101, 104–5, 108; fourth 2–3; marker 2, 8, 33, 38, 47, 52, 54, 71–2, 76, 84, 97–8, 108; overview 1–3; realization 6, 28, 57, 78, 106; second 1–3, 7, 33, 36–8, 40–1, 45, 49–52, 59, 62–5, 67–9, 75, 80–1, 83, 98, 105–6, 108; system 5–7, 9, 21, 31,

120 *Index*

34–6, 39, 46, 48–9, 53–4, *55*, 57, 85, 92, 95–7, 99–107, 109; third 1–3, 7, 31, 33–4, 39–41, 45, 49–54, 58–9, 62, 67–8, 75, 77, 81, 83–4, 105–6, 108
phonology 10, 12, 21–2, 97; or graphology 5, 21–2, 70
phylogenesis *see* semogenesis
polarity 53, 92, *93*
possessiveness 3, 5, 25, 44, 45, 80–2
Prague School 10–11
process 5, 7, 11, 24–5, 29, 31, 58–9, 66–7, 69–70, 74–5, 83, 86–7, 89–90, 94, 95, 100–2, 105
pronominality *see* nominality
pronoun 2, 7, 30, 39–41, 44, 49–52, *55*, 60–2, 65–6, 69–70, 72, 74–5, 77, 79–84, 96, 98–9, 106–7; demonstrative 2, 32, 46; dependent 74, 99; emphatic 47–8; indefinite 32; independent 75, 83–4, 99, 103n2, 107; interrogative 32; personal 1–2, 5–8, 18, 28–9, 31–5, 40, 44–9, 53–4, 57, 59, 65, 69, 71–84, 97–9, 104–7; possessive 3, 44, 45, 80–2; reciprocal 32; reflective 32, 45–7, 74; relative 31–2, 46; suffix 99
prosody 12–13, 47, *48,*
proximity 51–2, *55*, 104

quality 7, 26, 68

rank 6, 8, 15, 23–4, 49, 73, 75, 95, 100, 103
realization 5–8, 14, 17, *18,* 21–3, 25–6, 28, 31, 33, 49, 53–4, 57, 59, 76, 78, 83, 88, *93*, 94, 96, 99, 101–6, 108; rule, or statement 14–16, 24
reference 2, 30–1, 34, 36, 49, 51, 57, 59–62, 68, 70, 79, 83, 95; deictic 1, 104
referent 1–2, 7, 46, 79, 84, 96
reflexivity 2, 3, 5, 7, 29, 44–7, 104
relator 44
relexicogrammaticalization 95
Romance languages 74, 100–2, 108

Sanskrit 3, 35, 43
Saussure, F. de 10–12, 89
semantics 10, 14, 18, 20–22, 29, 57, 70, 85, *95*, 97; semantic features 5, 7, 28, 49, 80, 102
semogenesis 9–10, 90–2, 99, 102, 109
sentence 4, 13, 16, 27, 37, 56n1, 99
Spanish 35, 41, 44–5, 47, 49, 69–70, 73, 75, 83, 84n8, 98, 100–1, 107–8
speaker 2, *30*, 36–7, 41, 43, 49, 52, 60, 66–7, 76–7, 80, 86, 90, 98

speech 1–3, 38, 61, 73, 106; event 1, 104, 107; function 96; part of 3; role 1, 6–7, 30; sound 22
stratification 5, 21–2, 92
stratum 5, 6, 8, 10, 21–2, 70, 86, 92, 94, 105
structure 4–5, 7, 11–14, 16, 18–19, 21–4, 26–30, 43, 47, 53–4, 64, 70, 77, 86–9, 94, 100, 101, 104, 106, 109
suffix 35, 44–5, 47, 49–50, 52, 74–5, 81, 83, 94, 99, 103n3, 106–7
Swedish 15, 39
syntagmatic relation 4, 10–11, 13, 20, 87–8
system 4–7, 9–26, 29, 31, *32, 34,* 35–9, *41,* 42–3, 48–9, *50,* 53–4, *55,* 57, 62, 75, 77–8, 85–93, 95–107, 109; network 5–7, 13, 16–21, 23–5, 29–32, 34, 36, 38, 40–1, 43, 46, 48, 50–2, 54, 88–90, *93*, 104; semantic 6–7, 18, 105
Systemic Functional Linguistics (SFL) 4–8, 10, 18–21, 27–8, 30, 58, 68, 70, 85–7, 90–2, 95, 102–4, 107–9; *see also* Systemic Linguistics
Systemic Linguistics 10, 13, 14, 19–21, 28
systemic syntax *see* Hudson, R. A.

Tagalog 53, 102
tenor 25, 30, 62, 101, 108
tense 3, 5, 15, 54, 71, 74–5, 94, 95, 106
theme 5, 53, 102
topicality 53, 104
topology 88–9, *91*, 107–8
transitivity 3, 5, 23–5, 29, 100
Tucker, G. H. 26
typology 8, 36, 40, 57, 82–3, 85, 88–9, *91*, 98–100, 102–8

unit 3–6, 10, 13–14, 16, 20, 24–6, 33–4, 36, 94; phonematic 12–13
utterance 1–2, 12, 15, 30, 57, 67, 106

verb 3, 7, 25, 32, 35, 42, 44, 47, 49, 53–4, 57, 59, 66–9, 71, 73–5, 77, 83, 94, 98, 105, 107–8; honorific and humble 67, 107
verbal group 73
vocative 62–4, 68, 106
voice 3, 74

Whorf, B. L. 10–11

Yi Language 33

zero form 7, 72, 76–8, 84, 97–8, 105–6; categories 77